ICE SKATING FUNDAMENTALS

Second Edition

Marylin G. House

Ohio State University

KENDALL/HUNT PUBLISHING COMPANY
4050 Westmark Drive   Dubuque, Iowa 52002

Contents

Preface

After teaching ice skating for the past 15 years to students in Physical Education classes and to other students of all ages in classes or individually, I am more than ever convinced that ice skating is a pursuit that has something beneficial to offer to a great many people. Furthermore these 15 years have provided me with an ever increasing amount of evidence to indicate that anyone who really wants to, can learn to skate and skate well. It has been my pleasure to be instrumental in the learning process of many. This book has been written as a supplementary guide to introduce students to the activity, provide information about equipment and to present in a step by step fashion the basic skills of skating with techniques for developing these skills to the highest level of performance characterized by stability, control, speed, power and efficiency.

This second edition has been expanded to include a section on Elementary Figure Skating Skills suitable for advanced beginners.

SKATING

means
different
things

to
different

PEOPLE

Chapter I

Ice Skating—Fun, Challenge and Exercise for You

Ever since some enterprising caveman hit upon the idea of tying bone runners to his feet, the human species has been involved in the intriguing process of ice skating. Modern humans no less than the primitives are still captivated by the feeling of freedom associated with this manner of movement. Over the years there has evolved a variety of skating activities. Currently, the skating sports include hockey, figure skating and speed skating. Each of these requires a special type of skate (fig. 1), a particular set of skills and a unique training program. However, all three are based upon certain fundamental skills of balance and movement on the ice, and it is with these fundamentals that this book is concerned. Just as you must learn to stand before you walk, so you must learn to skate before you jump, play hockey or race. If you master the fundamentals presented here, you will have a firm foundation for going on into any one of the three skating sports, or for continued enjoyment of skating as a lifetime recreation.

ANSWERS TO SOME GENERAL QUESTIONS

What Has Skating to Offer the Participants?

Skating offers you challenge, fun and camaraderie. As recreation, it is a lifetime sport that can be pursued at any age. It can be done in a vigorous or leisurely fashion. The pace is set by you (not by your opponent as in tennis, or your teammates as in team sports). It offers opportunities for friendship, but it can be done alone. The skill itself can be used in a variety of ways, but in addition other avenues of interest may open up for you. You might be drawn toward officiating in hockey, or toward judging in figure skating, or toward one of the many facets of show skating (performance, choreography, costuming, lighting, etc.) or possibly toward rink management, teaching or coaching. With skating there are always new things to learn, new people to meet, new ideas to interest you and new directions to explore.

What Kinds of Skating Are There?

Skating today encompasses a wide variety of experiences for both the participant and the spectator. In general, skating activities can be grouped into three distinct areas . . . recreation, sport and entertainment.

1

Recreational Skating

A visit to any pond or rink is sufficient to reveal the festive air that pervades the atmosphere wherever people gather together to skate for fun. The gaiety and freedom that somehow seem inherent in skating make it naturally a very social pastime. Partner and trio skating are not only fun in themselves, but also spontaneous generators of a friendly climate. People of all ages enjoy skating as a marvelous recreation that provides hours of pleasure and healthful exercise.

The cost of recreational skating is relatively inexpensive (average admission is far less than the cost of a movie). The cost of equipment, instruction and club memberships is comparable to costs in other individual sports such as tennis or golf.

Skating as Sport

The three skating sports are speed skating, figure skating and hockey. All three are now Olympic sports and have their own national and international organizations to regulate their activities.

Since races always involve only forward skating in a counterclockwise direction, the skills involved in speed skating are relatively uncomplicated, utilizing only a few basic strokes. Training and effort must be directed toward development of power, speed and endurance. The speed skater uses a special skate which has a long, flat and very thin blade (fig. 1) to give a maximum amount of pushing surface and flow and a minimum of friction.

Speed skating for men has been included in the Olympics since 1924 and for women since 1960. Currently Olympic competition is held in the following events: Men—500 meters, 1500 meters, 5000 meters, 10,000 meters; women—500 meters, 1,000 meters, 1,500 meters and 3,000 meters. The USA has produced olympic champions in both men's and women's events. One of the most memorable, Eric Heiden, won gold medals in three of the men's events in 1980.

Good skating skills are absolutely essential in the game of Ice Hockey. Players need to have total mastery over all of the basic strokes and stops. Starting and stopping quickly and changing directions suddenly are vital parts of the play. Once the player has perfected his skating skills he must learn the art of stick handling and shooting as well as the intricacies and strategy of the game. The hockey skater also has specialized equipment. The blade is shorter and more sharply curved at the ends while being fairly flat in the center. This permits quick turning and generally better maneuverability. Modern hockey began in Canada and became an Olympic sport for men in 1920. The USA has produced two championship teams thus far in 1960 and 1980.

Figure Skating endeavors to blend the athletic quality of skating skill with the artistic dimensions of music and dance. Training is directed toward mastery of all the basic strokes, edges, figures, turns, jumps and spins as well as toward the development of a wide variety of special movements (lifts and

2

throw jumps for example for pair skaters) culminating in the achievement of an individual artistic "style" on the ice. The blade of the figure skate has a set of teeth or picks at the front to use for jumps and spins. Figure Skating became an Olympic Sport in 1908. Presently Olympic competition is held in singles for men and women, and in pairs and dance skating. The USA has had both men and women olympic champions in singles skating, but never as yet champions in the pairs or dance events.

Skating as Entertainment

With the advent of television, sport has become a major source of world-wide entertainment. Professional hockey now pays its players hundreds of thousands of dollars yearly to be a part of this entertainment. Figure skaters also are well paid to join skating shows that tour the world.

The entertainment picture embraces not only the professionals in sports but many amateurs as well. Figure skating and speed skating competitions on the national and international levels are televised routinely and it is probably only a matter of time until collegiate hockey will be televised as regularly as collegiate football and basketball.

The sum total of all of this publicity has been to stimulate even greater interest in skating and to provide additional professional careers for skilled skaters.

Is It Hard to Learn to Skate?

For most people, skating is not hard to learn. It requires an average amount of coordination to maintain balance. After fifteen hours on the ice, the average person will be able to skate forward, backward, stop and turn around with a fair amount of confidence.

Should a Beginner Seek Instruction?

Yes. It need not be private instruction . . . a class will do nicely for most beginners. It is easier to learn a skill correctly from the beginning than to have to correct errors later. Good instruction can help reduce the hazards associated with the beginner's fear of falling. It is therefore helpful from the viewpoint of safety.

Is Skating Hazardous?

No. Compared to other sports skating is relatively safe. However, ice like water, is potentially dangerous and deserves respect. THE FOLLOWING SAFETY PRECAUTIONS SHOULD BE OBSERVED.

For the first few times on the ice stay near the barrier until you can stop easily.

If possible obtain some form of instruction the first few times that you skate.

3

SKATING
is

FUN
at

ANY
AGE!

> *Keep knees relaxed, bent, and forward (covering toes) . . . never stiff*
> *or locked.*
> *Learn to relax when you fall and get up quickly.*
> *Watch where you are going . . . always! Observe all traffic patterns.*

What is the Best Age for Starting to Skate?

Whenever the desire is there. Special care must be taken to see that young children are equipped with properly fitted boots. Elderly people who take up skating should be reasonably cautious and probably should try to have private instruction for their first few times on the ice.

Is Skating Expensive?

Unless you are planning a career in competitive figure skating, you will find that the expenses involved in skating are quite moderate. Equipment generally is less than that for skiing or golf. There are no travel expenses involved. Instruction is no more costly than that in tennis or skiing. Rink admissions vary of course, but run considerably less on the whole than the price of a movie ticket. If you skate with a club your dues will run higher than the public sessions, but not more so than other comparable sport clubs. For a moderate investment you should be able to reap ample profits in terms of hours of enjoyment, pleasure and friendships from this healthful lifetime sport.

ORIGINS OF SKATING

Skating as a method of locomotion and transport is very old. Primitive bone skates unearthed in Northern Europe and England indicate that as far back as 2000 B.C. men were navigating on bone runners over ice. *Bone skates would slide, but had no edges with which to grip the ice, so poles had to be used for propulsion and steering.* Bone skates were used in some parts of Europe and England right up into the middle ages. There is a reference to an iron skate in early Scandinavian literature dating its use to around 200 A.D. about the time that general use of iron became widespread.

The first iron skates were constructed as wide strips fastened to wooden blocks which were strapped to the feet. The development of a bladed skate is thought to have occurred in the Netherlands, where the frozen canals provided long distances of ice surface relatively free of heavy snows. These canals provided a link, and were sometimes the only avenue of communication between villages during the winters, so that the incentive to navigate over the ice was strong.

The development of a bladed skate meant that the skater no longer had to depend on a pole for pushing and steering. He was able to use the edges of the blade to grip the ice and push against it. The Dutch discovered the natural way of stroking by using edges. A clue as to when the bladed skate came into use is given by a wood engraving (1498 A.D. Holland) by Brugman which portrays an accident on the ice in which a young girl has fallen. The girl is wearing bladed skates and the other skaters in the picture appear to be stroking in a manner similar to our modern method.

While the primary impetus for early skaters was the practical matter of transportation, it wasn't long till a more frivolous aspect began to evolve. With the advent of bladed skates and the use of edges, the element of speed in skating was greatly enhanced, and it was only a matter of time until skaters experimented to see how fast they could go individually and then collectively in the form of racing. *In Holland by the sixteenth century speed skating was well developed and organized.* Both men and women competed for prizes and honors before crowds of people. Then as now skaters and spectators enjoyed the excitement of racing competition.

Dutch paintings of the seventeenth century give evidence, that by that time, skating in Holland had become an important recreation for all of the people . . . peasants to princes . . . and it was spreading to other countries. *When the aristocracy took an interest in skating, their interest centered on elegant style and artistic skating rather than on speed.* This shift in focus away from speed to form, style and creativeness gradually led to the evolution of the sport of figure skating. At this point it was not the Dutch but the English who made the next significant contributions.

Skating in England developed more as a recreation than a necessary mode of transportation. It was pursued on small surfaces like ponds rather than on large expanses of ice like the canals of Holland. It soon became apparent that the long, low, flat skates of the Dutch made for traveling long distances on ice, were totally unsatisfactory on ponds where turns and circles within a small radius were constantly being attempted. The English developed the first figure skate early in the eighteenth century. Its essential features included a short curved blade with a high stanchion . . . harder to balance on (especially since it stopped short of the heel) but much easier to turn on. The introduction of this blade greatly accelerated the development of figure skating.

Early figure skaters were almost entirely preoccupied with making tracings on the ice. Competitions were held to encourage the invention of new complex figures. Everything was tried from the letters of the alphabet to intricate filigree designs of stars.

Meanwhile skating was spreading to more and more people. The English tended to take more interest in the technique and science of skating, focusing their attention more on figures, while elsewhere, especially in Paris, the focus was on style, elegance and beauty of movement. Skating clubs were springing up in many countries. The first was formed in Edinburgh, Scotland (1742). The United States did not have its first skating club until 1849 in Philadelphia.

Modern figure skating as we know it was introduced by Jackson Haines . . . an American. Haines was trained in ballet, but he taught physical culture as well as ballet and performed as an exhibition skater and juggler. Haines conceived of skating as an art form. He brought to it the drama and theatricality of dance. He wore colorful costumes and used musical accompaniment for his skating routines. He developed a skate that was much safer because it clamped directly to the boot. This skate was also stronger, permitting jumping of much greater athletic quality than before. Haines style of skating was rejected in America and Britain, but the Europeans, especially the Viennese, understood and accepted his ideals in skating. A Viennese school of skating evolved composed of his pupils, and followers gradually spread his methods and ideas throughout the skating world.

In 1892 the International Skating Union was formed, and in 1896 the first amateur international skating competition was held. Initially women had no special competitions. In 1902 Mrs. Madge Syers of England nearly beat Ulrich Salchow the defending champion. In 1906 separate events for women were initiated.

Next to Jackson Haines the skater having the greatest impact on modern figure skating was Sonja Henie. She won the World Championship in her home town of Olso in 1927 at the age of thirteen. She was the first "child" champion and started the trend toward earlier participation. Her style was vigorous and athletic for that period. She introduced the short skirt for women skaters that allowed them the freedom of movement necessary for athletic skating. Sonja was ten times the World Champion, and three times the Olympic Champion. Her spectacular record in competitive skating greatly stimulated interest in amateur competition. However, her greatest contribution was made after she left amateur competition and took up a career as a professional skater. She toured the United States with her show and her career culminated with a series of movies which made the art of skating known and seen in every corner of the world.

The most important figure in the recent history of skating is Dick Button. He was the first to bring to skating most of the double and triple jumps. He refocused attention on the athletic possibilities within the sport and greatly changed free skating by augmenting the repertoire of athletic feats. *Button was the first American to win an Olympic Gold Medal in skating. He was World Champion five times and Olympic Champion twice.*

Contemporary figure skating particularly amateur competition is still dominated by a strong emphasis on jumping. Triple jumps are becoming common and there are skaters who have done quadruple revolution jumps. There is however, another interesting trend visible in both amateur and professional ranks. This is the trend toward artistry in skating. It is best exemplified by

Toller Cranston and John Curry. Cranston is a canadian who in the 70's introduced a whole new style of skating into the world of amateur competition. He expanded the repetoire of movements acceptable on the ice borrowing many of them from modern dance. He banished forever the narrow concept that only balletic, flowing movements should be used in free skating. He re-emphasized the importance of musical interpretation and opened up whole new areas of expression highlighting the value of originality in free skating. British John Curry was the 1976 Olympic champion. Although their styles of skating are totally different, both men are strong exponents of musical interpretation and see skating as an expressive art form. They have both formed their own skating performance companies. Curry has had numbers choreographed for himself and his company by some of the leading contemporary dance choreographers. Unfortunately there is not a very large audience appreciative of this type of skating, and at present both companies have had to disband. It is to be hoped that the recent upsurge of professional skating competitions which are geared toward artistic skating may help to educate audiences and develop more interest in skating as an art form.

Ice hockey appears to be the youngest of the skating sports. Although its ancient origin probably dates back to antiquity in the form of field hockey, the modern form of the game originated in Canada around 1855. It became an Olympic sport in 1920.

* * * * *

Supplemental Readings

History of Skating—
Brown, Nigel—1959— "A History of Ice Skating", Barnes Company, Inc., New York, N.Y.
Goodfellow, Arthur T.—1972— "Wonderful World of Skates", A. T. Goodfellow Publisher, Mountainsburg, Arkansas 72946.

Figure Skating—
Fassi, Carlo—1980— "Figure Skating with Carlo Fassi", Charles Scribner's Sons, New York, N.Y.
Ogilvie, Robert—1969— "Basic Ice Skating Skills" United States Figure Skating Association, Colorado Springs, Colorado.
Owen, Maribel Vinson—1972— "The Fun of Figure Skating", Harper and Brother, New York, N.Y.
USFA—Official Rule Book—(Current Year) United States Figure Skating Association, Colorado Springs, Colorado.

Hockey

Meeker, Howie—1973— "Howie Meeker's Hockey Basics", Prentice Hall—Canada Ltd., Scarborough, Ontario.

Wild, John—1970— "Power Skating—Key to Better Hockey", Prentice Hall—Canada Ltd., Scarborough, Ontario.

Chapter II

Equipment—Choice, Use and Maintenance

TYPES OF SKATES

When we speak of skates we are referring to the combination of a pair of skating boots attached to a pair of blades: SKATES = BOOTS + BLADES. There are three types of skates: *speed skates, hockey skates* and *figure skates* (Fig. 1). All good quality skates regardless of type have boots with a built-in support in the instep. This built-in support is known as a *counter* (Fig. 3). All blades regardless of type have a bottom which is curved from front to back. This curve is known as the *rocker* of the blade.

Every skate blade has two edges running along either side of the bottom. The edge nearer to the inside of the boot (big toe side) is the inside edge and the one nearer the outside of the boot (little toe side) is the outside edge. Both hockey and figure blades are hollow ground in the sharpening process. This means that the width of the blade is concavely curved making the edges more distinct and sharp. The speed skate is too narrow to hollow grind.

Each type of skate has unique features related to its function.

Figure Skates

Boot —
Strong construction—double or triple layer of good quality leather

Long counter—extends from heel to just behind joint of big toe (Fig. 3).

Thick sole—raised heel 1–1½ inches

Blade —
Length of blade extends beyond heel of boot, toe picks at front

Relatively gradual rocker—no flat area

Wide blade (³⁄₁₆ inch)

Low solid stanchions

Attached by screws

The strong sturdy construction of the boot and the long counter provide good support for jumps, spins and strong edges. The thick soles allow the blade to be attached by screws and to be moved to suit the skaters balance. The picks assist in jumps and spins. The gradual rocker allows a greater range in balance placement. The low solid stanchions provide greater blade strength for jump landings. This is the easiest skate to learn on.

11

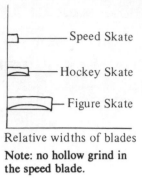

Relative widths of blades

Note: no hollow grind in the speed blade.

Speed Skate
Blade is extra long and very thin and flat. Boot is lightweight and low cut.

Figure Skate
Blade has a very gradual curve—no completely flat area, picks at front. Width is twice that of hockey blade. Boot has thick sole and heel—very sturdy construction.

Hockey Skate
Blade is flat in middle but curves sharply at front and back. Width is twice that of speed skate. Boot has tendon guard in back—heavy construction.

Figure 1. Types of skates.

12

Hockey Skates

Boot
{
Heavy construction of leather or plastic—long counter extends completely under arch of foot (Fig. 3)
Hard toes
Thin soles—slightly raised heel ¼–½ inch thick padded tendon guard built in to back top of boot.
}

Blade
{
Length of blade nearly equal to length of boot, width = ⅛ inch
Rocker—sharp at front and back and relatively flat in middle of blade
Riveted on thin sole
}

The hard toes, heavy construction and tendon guards all help to protect the player from damage by the fast travelling puck or sticks of other players. The heavy construction also provides good support. The shorter blade with sharp rocker at front and back allows quick turning and good maneuverability, while the relatively narrow width and center flat portion promote flow (reduce friction) for efficient movement.

Speed Skates

Boot
{
Light weight soft leather
Very short counter (Fig. 3)
Low cut tops
Very thin sole—no raised heel
}

Blade
{
Very long—extends beyond toe and heel
Very thin—about ¹⁄₁₆ inch wide
Very little rocker except at front
Light weight tubular construction
Riveted on thin sole
May be offset to the left (races always go in a counter-clockwise direction only)
}

The long thin blade offers the skater more pushing length and less friction. The low light weight boot helps reduce load and conserve energy. Speed skates are impractical to learn on unless you have a very large outdoor lake or rink to skate on. Most indoor rinks do not have any rental speed skates and many rinks will not allow them to be used during public sessions.

BUYING SKATES

The value of having your own equipment can hardly be over stated. As soon as possible try to buy your own skates. It is an enormous help to have the same good properly fitting equipment everytime you are on the ice. If you are learning to skate in order to play hockey, then learn on hockey skates.

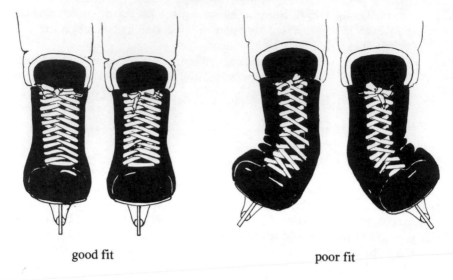

good fit   poor fit

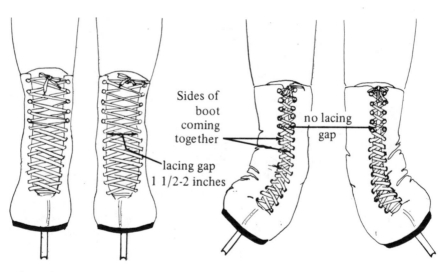

good fit   poor fit

Figure 2. Good fitting boots are snug with no wrinkles over the ankles and with a wide lacing gap. Poor fitting boots are too large—ankles fall in—lacing gap is narrow or missing—boot wrinkles over ankles.

Otherwise it is best to learn on figure skates, because the boots give more support, the blades are wider and the transition to hockey or speed skates is relatively easy. In addition you can learn to jump, spin and dance on ice . . . none of which can be done easily on hockey skates.

The best insurance for getting good quality skates that fit you properly is to buy them in an ice skating rink at the "pro" shop. (Stay away from department stores and sporting goods stores even though the prices might be a few dollars lower. Their merchandise is frequently inferior, and they seldom employ persons who know how to fit you properly). The lowest priced sets available at rinks are fine for youngsters with rapidly growing feet, but if your feet are no longer changing size, it is wiser to invest in a more expensive and durable pair.

For a beginner the most important part of the skate is the boot. Almost any blade is adequate for a year or so, if it is mounted properly and correctly sharpened. A wise beginner will invest in as good a boot as he/she can afford. Hockey skates are sold as units, boots and blades already attached, but for better quality figure skates boots and blades are sold separately. *The following features are the most important ones to check when you buy skates—hockey or figure.*

1. *Good support in the boot—*
   Make sure the boot has a *strong counter* (Fig. 3) running from heel to the front border of the instep. It will be a little longer in figure boots.
   Sturdy construction of tops—Figure boots should have double or triple layer of good quality leather. *Hockey boots*—even heavier construction of tops of either leather or plastic with hard toes and tendon guards.
2. *Good fit of boot—*
   Your boot should fit snugly, over a *thin sock,* so that it can provide you with maximum support. It will stretch with wear. Skating boots tend to run larger than street shoes. You will probably wear one to two full sizes smaller than your street shoes. Try on several sizes and widths. Choose the ones that fit most closely without pinching. *The fit should be snug enough in the back so that the heel can't raise up,* and *roomy enough in front to allow your toes to wiggle* . . . this helps maintain circulation and keep the feet warm. There should be *no wrinkles in the leather over the ankle bones. There should be a gap of 1½" to 2" between the sides of the boot where the tongue lacings go* (Fig. 2). Remember, a snug fitting boot is the beginner's greatest ally. *Since it will stretch with wear,* don't be afraid to start out with something that feels a bit tight compared to your street shoe. Keep in mind the fact that *when you skate you do not bend your foot in the middle as you do when walking, so the fit can be quite snug and yet comfortable.*

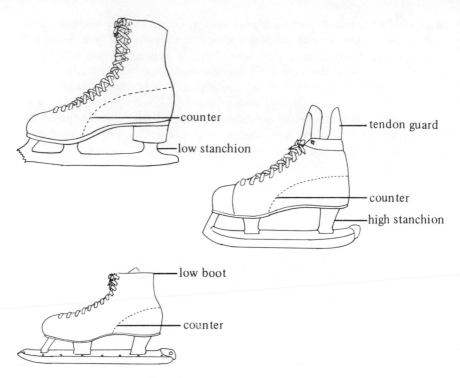

Figure 3. Skate structure. *Top:* figure skate has longest counter, lowest stanchions; *Middle:* hockey skate has high stanchions, good counter, tendon guard; *Bottom:* speed skate has short counter.

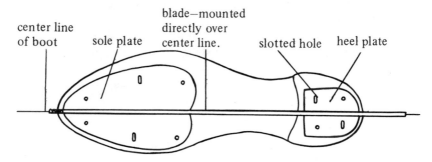

Figure 4. Blade mounting. Blade must be mounted parallel to the center line of boot (see appendix for determination of center line). Sole and heel plate should come to within an eighth of an inch of the ends of the boot.

You can expect new boots to feel stiff and tight for a while. As you wear them the leather will soften and shape to your feet. Use thin sponge rubber pads over ankle bones or any other place where the pressure of the new stiff leather creates soreness. Wear boots for only short periods the first few times if they are hurting your feet.

3. *Size of Blade*

   The length of the blade from the tip of the sole plate to the tip of the heel plate *should be equal to, or not more than ¼ inch shorter* than the length of the boot. (Fig. 4)

4. *Placement of Blade* (Fig. 4)

   The *blades should be mounted in a straight line that parallels the main axis of the boot.** Hockey blades must be riveted on because of the thin sole, so checking their placement is especially important since they cannot be moved. Figure blades should be *screwed on, not riveted.* This permits you to change the position of the blade and adjust it to your balance. If you are buying separate boots and blades try to get blades with slotted holes. Have the blades mounted with only 4 screws (in the slotted holes) and try them on the ice before deciding on final placement and adding the other screws. Before having the blade mounted permanently, apply a double coat of varnish to the sole of the boot to waterproof it. (This should be repeated every year).

5. *Quality of Blade*

   The quality of the blades varies almost directly with the price and is a reflection of the quality of the steel. *For a beginner, the blade quality is not crucial.* What is most important about the blade is that it is correctly mounted as described above and properly sharpened** with even edges.

RENTING SKATES

Most rinks have both hockey and figure skates that you may rent. Since the rental skates are worn by many people they are usually pretty stretched out and may not provide very good support. You may find that you wear a size and a half to two sizes smaller than your street shoe. Follow the instructions given previously concerning fit of boot when buying skates. Ask for the newest pair that they have in your size to get a pair with better support. If you cannot get a good fit in a rental skate, it is even more important to try to buy some skates of your own as soon as you can.

*See Appendix C
**See Appendix D

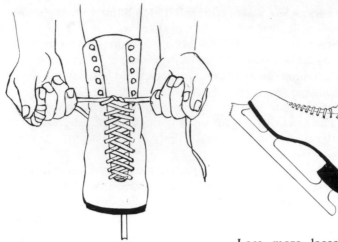

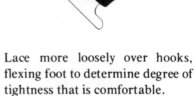

Twist laces to hold firmness over instep and ankle.

Lace more loosely over hooks, flexing foot to determine degree of tightness that is comfortable.

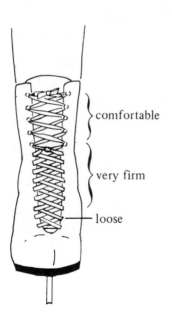

comfortable

very firm

loose

Tuck ends of laces in top of boots.

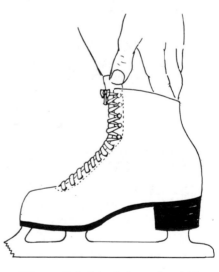

When all finished there should be room for two fingers in back of boot at top. Hockey boots can be tighter at top.

Figure 5. Skate lacing.

USE AND CARE OF EQUIPMENT

Lacing Your Boots

In order to obtain maximum support and comfort from your boots it is necessary to lace them properly. First of all make sure that the tongue of the boot is well pulled up and centered. Lace loose enough in the first two holes so toes can wiggle (this keeps the circulation going and the feet warm)

Figure Boots:

Lace firmly (not too tight or it will cut off circulation) up over the arch to the hole just below the ankle bone (remember that this is the area that needs the most support). Twist laces around each other at this point to keep them from slipping. Lace more loosely up the remaining holes or hooks flexing the foot as you do so to make sure it is not too tight. Tuck laces into the top of the boot and use a double knot so that they will not unravel. When you are through you should be able to insert two fingers in the back of the boot at the top (Fig. 5). If your laces are drawn too tightly at the top of the boot, you will not be able to bend your knees enough and you may get cramps in your calf muscles.

Hockey Boots:

Hockey boots are cut shorter than figure boots and have a heavier construction plus the tendon guard in back. Because of these features the boots are laced firmly all the way from toes to top.

Care of Equipment

Use a leather conditioner to clean and soften your boots. Use shoe polish sparingly . . . it has a tendency to cause the leather to crack. *Have your blades sharpened when necessary.** This will depend on how often you skate, where you skate (an outdoor pond means lots more sharpening than indoor skating), the quality of the steel and your own preference. A minimum would be once a season for a skater who skates several times a week on indoor ice.

When you are going to or from the ice be sure that you walk only where there is rubber matting or wood, *NEVER walk on cement with unprotected blades.* Rubber or wooden skate guards can be purchased and worn to protect blades when walking to and from the ice.

When you have finished skating, *dry the blades thoroughly* with a chamois or soft towel and *check the blades for any loose or missing screws.* A bag for carrying your skates or a locker at the rink in which to keep them will be a helpful convenience. *Do not store blades with guards on.* The moisture condensation will cause them to rust. A towel or chamois in the bottom of your locker or skate bag makes an ideal place to set your skates between sessions.

*See Appendix D

EQUIPMENT CHECK LIST

Boots

Snug Fit—
> heel cannot lift up
> lacing gap 1½–2 inches wide
> no wrinkles over ankles

Sturdy Construction—
> double or triple layer of leather
> strong built-in counter in arch
> sponge rubber or felt padding on tongue

Special
> Hockey boots
> built in tendon guards at back
> hard toes
> strong leather or plastic

Blades

Length
> not more than ¼ inch shorter than sole of boot

Placement
> parallel to or on center axis of boot

Figure Blades
> should be screwed on bottom, four slotted holes

Sharpening
> hollow ground
> no nicks or burrs
> even edges

Extra
> Guards—to protect blades when walking to or from ice
> Chamois—for careful drying of blades
> Leather conditioner (instead of softener)—to preserve boots
> Clear varnish—to coat soles of boots yearly
> Skate bag—

Chapter III

How to Begin

SAFETY CONSIDERATIONS

As mentioned earlier skating is a relatively safe activity. A few basic cautions should be obeyed.

1. OBSERVE ALL TRAFFIC PATTERNS.
2. WATCH WHERE YOU ARE GOING—ESPECIALLY WHEN SKATING BACKWARDS.
3. FOREIGN OBJECTS ON THE ICE ARE A HAZARD, SO BE SURE THAT YOU DON'T DROP ANYTHING SUCH AS KLEENEX, BUTTONS, HAIR PINS, ETC.
4. DON'T EAT ON THE ICE—DON'T CHEW GUM WHILE SKATING.
5. DON'T SIT ON RINK BARRIER.
6. DON'T FIGHT A FALL. RELAX AND 'GO WITH IT' THEN GET UP QUICKLY (TO THE KNEES FIRST).
7. PERFORM A FEW SIMPLE WARM-UP EXERCISES BEFORE PUTTING ON SKATES TO GET BODY READY FOR SKATING.*
8. OBTAIN EQUIPMENT THAT FITS PROPERLY AND HAS ADEQUATE SUPPORT. LACE BOOTS CORRECTLY FOR MAXIMUM SUPPORT.

OFF-ICE PREPARATIONS

Before you put your skates on take a look at the structure of the blade. Notice that its shape (front to back) is curved on the bottom like a rocker rather than flat. Because of this rocker type bottom only a portion of the blade is in contact with the ice when you skate. That portion may shift along the length of the blade as you skate. The least stable areas will be at either end. *A major objective in learning to skate is to keep your balance centered over the middle area of the blade.*

After putting the skates on (see chapter II for choosing and lacing skates) walk around a bit in the warming room to get the feel of the skates. If your ankles feel wobbly and keep falling in (or out) try a smaller or narrower size boot.

Stand still with your feet 10 to 12 inches apart, head up, back straight, hands out to sides at hip height and slightly in front of the line of the shoulders, knees straight. Now bend your knees and bring them forward till they cover your toes (so that looking down you can't see your feet). We will call this the

*See Appendix B

21

6.1. Side view

6.2. KEY POSTURE in
stroking position

6.3. Front view

Figure 6. The "KEY POSTURE".

"KEY POSTURE" (Fig. 6) for good skating. In this posture the feet, hips and shoulders are all facing straight ahead along the path of travel. The term 'square' is used to describe this relationship. Thus we say the feet, shoulders and hips are square to each other.

THE KNEES OVER TOES POSITION IS AN IMPORTANT PART OF THIS KEY POSTURE FOR THE FOLLOWING REASONS:

1. Bending the knees lowers the skater's center of gravity**, and thereby increases stability.
2. Knee bend centers the skater's weight over the middle of the blades by bringing the line of gravity** close to the center of the base of support increasing stability.
3. Knee bend provides the power for pushing against the ice with the edge of the blade as the leg extends in the thrust.
4. Knee flexibility provides the body with the quickest most efficient way of reacting and controlling changes in balance.

Before going on the ice it is good to explore the edges of the blades. Assume the KEY POSTURE position then let the ankles turn in slightly until you feel the blades go over on the inside edges. Next, bring ankles straight so weight is on the width of the blades (this is known as the "flat" of the blade . . . actually you are on both edges simultaneously). Finally, let ankles turn out slightly to feel outside edges of the blades. It is possible to skate on either outside or inside edges of the blades or on the flat. When you go on the ice you can explore all three possibilities.

GETTING YOUR BALANCE

Walking around in the warming room is useful in giving you an idea of how it feels to balance on the narrow blades and how to hold your ankles up straight. However, once you move to the ice it is different. Because of the reduced friction between the blades and the ice it is harder to keep your feet under you. Do not be embarrassed to make use of the rink barrier when you first step on the ice. Step on sideways to keep the skate from running away, then turn and face the barrier. *Holding on with both hands assume the KEY POSTURE (knees over toes) and rock forward until you find the front tips of the blades* (or picks if you are wearing figure skates). *Still holding on,* rock your weight to the back tips of the blades. Do this rocking forward and back several times to give yourself a feeling for the length and curvature of the blades.

**See Appendix A

 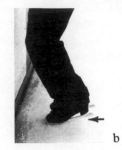 

a   b   c

Rocking: to feel the length and curve of the blade. (a) face barrier, hold on, knees over toes (b) rock weight to front tips of blades—lift heels. (c) rock weight to back tips of blades—left toes.

a   b   c

Barrier pull: to feel a balanced glide. (a) feet 10" apart, knees over toes, (b) even weight on both feet (c) use hand over hand pull to move along barrier.

a   b   c

Weight shifting: to feel support **leg bend** as it takes body **weight.** (a) **right knee bends, left leg pushes** (b) **left leg bends, right leg pushes** (c) turn toes out, pick up pushing foot.

Figure 7. Balance exercises.

Barrier Pull: Turn body and feet sideways to barrier. Assume the KEY POSTURE with feet on slight inside edges (weight evenly distributed on both feet). Use a hand over hand action to move yourself along the barrier so that you can feel yourself moving along in a balanced glide with the weight centered over the middle of both skates.

Weight Shifting: Moving along barrier in the KEY POSTURE (with inside hand on barrier if desired), shift the weight from one leg to the other by increasing the knee bend first in the right leg and then in the left leg. Simultaneously straighten the opposite leg as you push with the inside edge to the side. At first keep both feet on the ice, then progress to the point where you lift the straightening leg and finish the weight shift to the other leg. Continue to shift weight from foot to foot, but now turn toes outward. You will find yourself beginning to stroke. Be sure to pick up the whole blade quickly and completely each time after pushing. (If you pick up the heel first it will cause the toe pick to catch in the ice and you will develop a habit of 'picking' which is ruinous to good stroking.) Gradually try to lengthen the glide on one foot between pushes.

Static Balance—two feet: Stand still, assume the KEY POSTURE. Alternately bend and straighten knees without allowing feet to move. Hold weight over center of blades.

Static Balance—one foot: Most people are surprised to discover that they can balance rather well for considerable time on one foot. Assume KEY POSTURE—lift one foot and see how long you can remain on the other (you are allowed to move the foot you are balancing on).

FALLING

Falling is a natural part of skating. *The main thing when falling is to relax and go with the fall.* When the body is relaxed it responds with a reflex action and is seldom injured. In order to relieve the natural anxiety about falling, it is a good idea to do some practice falling. *It is probably safer to fall forward than backward, because the potential for serious damage to the body is less in a forward fall than in a backward fall.*

Let's take a moment to consider the reflex action of the body when it falls.

Forward Fall: If the body is relaxed it automatically flings the arms out and forward, stretches out full length and arches the back a little. Note how each reaction protects. The hands break the fall and slide out then the impact is widely distributed over the whole front

Practice fall—forward: (a) crouch down, hands on ice (b) slide hands forward, straighten knees (c) front of body contacts ice.

Practice fall—backward: (a) bend in middle, chest on knees, arms forward (b) lower seat to heels (c) slide feet forward.

Figure 8. Falling.

of the body which lessens the force on any one part. The stretching tends to straighten the knees and protect them and the slightly arched back protects the head, especially the chin.

Backward Fall: When the body starts to fall backward if it is relaxed it bends forward at the hips in a jackknife position and the arms are flung forward and the landing is made on the seat—like sitting in a chair. Note the forward bend of the upper body brings the head and tail bone to a safer position. The arms being forward is also a safer position because breaking a backward fall with the hands is hazardous since the hands will not slide out but rather tend to stay in place and take the full weight of the body.

Practice Falls: In order to relieve anxiety about falling it is a good idea to do some practice falling. Do the forward fall from a standstill and the backward fall while moving forward slowly on two feet. *Always get up quickly from a fall.—It is best to get to the knees first then push up with hands.* Even though *it is safer to fall forward than backward,* many people are so afraid of a forward fall that they throw their weight to the heels whenever they feel their balance tipping forward. If you detect this tendency in yourself it might be helpful to do a number of practice forward falls to help diminish your fear.

SNOW PLOW STOP

The braking action is effected by pushing the feet apart and turning the toes in so that the blades are skidding on slight inside edges.

Step 1. Start by facing barrier, feet together, about an arms length away. Bend knees and grasp barrier with hands, turn toes inward and push out on heels so feet move apart on slight inside edges. Pull in to barrier with arms . . . skates skidding and shaving ice surface with slight inside edges. If you have difficulty in getting the blades to slide you may be taking too much edge, try increasing the angle between the ice and the inner edge of the blade.

Step 2. Glide forward on two feet with feet fairly close together, knees bent . . . turn toes in and push heels out so that skates move apart with blades sliding or skidding on slight inside edges. Keep even pressure on both feet as the blades scrape the ice until you are completely stopped. Some people find it easier to learn a one foot snowplow stop. To try this proceed as for regular snowplow, but turn only one toe in and extend that foot forward ahead of the other as it shaves ice. Put more pressure on the front foot (back foot continues to go straight).

9.1.   9.2.

Figure 9.1. Snowplow stop—push heels out, slide on two inside edges; **9.2.** one foot snowplow stop.

27

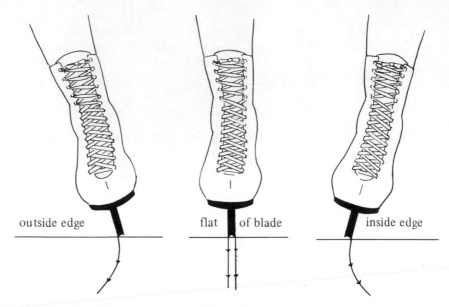

outside edge   flat   of blade   inside edge

Figure 10.

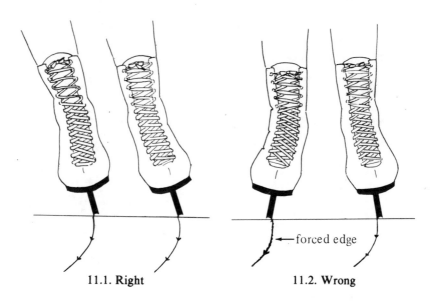

11.1. Right   11.2. Wrong

forced edge

Figure 11.

Chapter IV

Edges, Mechanics and Two-Footed Skating

EDGES

You are already acquainted with the fact that each skate blade has two edges running its length which are separated by a width of about ³⁄₁₆″ (figure blade) to ¹⁄₁₆″ (speed skate). You have seen and experienced how inside edges can be used for pushing against the ice to effect movement, and also how they can be used to effect a stop by scraping the ice as in the snowplow stop. In general, where you go on the ice will depend on what part of the blade you are on.

If you try to skate on the width or flat of your blade rather than on one of the edges, the blade will in fact be on both edges at once because of the hollow grind done in the sharpening. The direction of travel will be a straight line. (Fig. 10)

If you skate on the inside edge of the blade, the direction of travel will be a curve toward the side opposite to the foot you are on. Example—skating an inside edge on the right foot will take you on a curve to the left. (Fig. 10)

If you skate on an outside edge the direction of travel will be a curve in the same direction as the foot you are on. Example—a left outside forward edge will take you on a curve to the left.

If you travel on a curve on two feet, they will be on opposite edges. Example—curve to right—left foot is on inside edge, right foot is on outside edge. (Fig. 11.1)

If the feet are not on opposite edges when travelling on a curve, it will be necessary to 'force' the incorrect edge. This will cause increased friction, loss of flow and difficulty in staying on the curve. In (Fig. 11.2) the right foot is being forced around the curve on the wrong (inside) edge.

MECHANICS

There are a few basic principles taken from ordinary mechanics that are applicable to skating and skaters. It is helpful to be aware of these as they can be of considerable usefulness to you as you progress from skill to skill.

Stability

1. Relationship between balance and size of base of support. *The broader the base of support of an object the greater its stability and the easier it is to maintain balance.* Everyone knows that a book is more stable when it is lying down than when it is stood on end. The same is true of a skater. If your only goal on the ice was stability, then prone on the ice would be your best position (Fig. 12). However, it is not necessary to go to a ridiculous extreme to see the application of this principle to skating. The base of support on the ice will be your skate or skates. Two skates on the ice provide more base and therefore more stability than one. This base can be further enlarged by placing the feet apart. Thus by placing the feet ten to twelve inches apart the base is enlarged from $\frac{3}{16}$ inch (if you were only on one skate) to a foot wide. This would suggest that when you first start skating and are getting your balance, it will be easier to start with a broad base (i.e., two feet placed a distance apart) and gradually work down to one foot at a time. This applies to learning new skills also, such as backward skating, hockey stop, turns, etc.

2. Role of Center of Gravity

   The lower the center of gravity (cg) of an object the greater its stability. The cg can be defined as the point through which the resultant force of gravity acts on a body, or the point at which the entire weight of the body may be considered to be concentrated. In the human body the location of the center of gravity depends upon the individual anatomic structure as well as the position of the body parts. For a person of average build standing with arms at sides, the center of gravity is located in the pelvis. It tends to be slightly lower in women because of the wider, heavier pelvis and shorter legs.

   A bookcase with all of the books concentrated in the two lowest shelves would be much harder to tip over than one with books concentrated in the two top shelves. The lesson inherent here for the skater is that the lower to the ice that he can concentrate his weight (i.e. lower his cg) the greater will be his stability. There is a very quick and efficient way for the skater to lower his/her cg (other than falling) and that is by bending the knees. This method is relatively easy to control and it also contributes toward keeping the cg over the center of the skate.

Balance

Skating balance is of a dynamic rather than a static nature, which means that it is constantly changing. In terms of the skate blade it means that the point of balance is not fixed, but shifts continuously. The area over which this shifting can occur is normally limited to the central portion of the blade, the

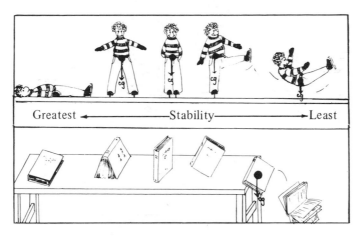

Figure 12. Factors affecting balance. Relationship between stability and size of support base, also relationship of center of gravity (e.g.) to base of support and stability.

closer you can keep your balance to the center of the blade the more stable you will be. Conversely the farther from center your balance wanders the less stable it will be.

The main question is—how can the body most easily and efficiently maintain a stable balance over the center of the skates?

We find that the answer rests upon the KEY POSTURE that you learned in Chapter II. The essential features of the KEY POSTURE are: 1) knees bent and brought forward to cover toes, 2) shoulders and hips level and facing directly forward, 3) hands out to the sides at hip height and slightly forward, 4) head erect, eyes forward, 5) back straight but a slight bend forward at the hips because of acceleration when moving (Fig. 13). The three main balance adjustment points are at the ankle, knee and hip. In stroking, where you are moving from one foot to the other, the support leg is bending as the pushing leg is straightening. (The arms may be more comfortable used in opposition to the pushing leg rather than held out to the sides.) THE ROLE PLAYED BY KNEE FLEXIBILITY IN SKATING IS CRUCIAL FOR THE FOLLOWING REASONS:

1. Knee bend provides the power for pushing against the ice when moving.
2. Bending the knees lowers the center of gravity and increases stability.
3. Knee bend plus ankle bend to bring the knee forward helps center the weight over the blade thereby increasing stability.
4. Knee flexibility provides the body with the quickest and most efficient way of reacting to and controlling changes in balance.

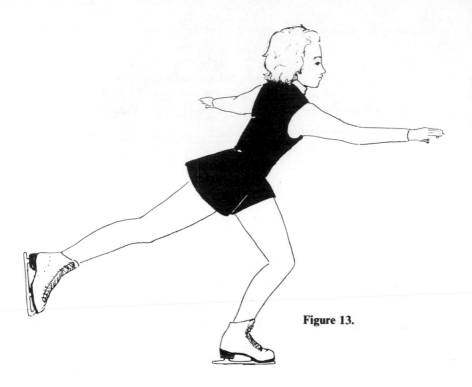

Figure 13.

Newton's Laws of Motion

Bodies moving on ice are subject to the same physical laws as moving bodies elsewhere.

First Law—A body at rest or in motion will remain at rest or in motion unless some external force is applied to it.

In skating, the external force to start and stop you (if it is to be under your control) must be applied by you, using your leg muscles to exert pressure through the edge of the blade against the ice. When you are trying to move yourself, the edge of the blade is used in a thrusting motion to the side and in the direction of travel, with the force being applied downward and in the opposite direction to that of travel. When you are trying to stop yourself, the blade is used to shave or scrape the surface of the ice in a direction perpendicular to that of travel. The shaving action results in greatly increased friction which then, is the actual force stopping you.

Second Law—The rate at which the momentum of a body changes is equal to the force acting and takes place in the direction of the straight line in which the resultant force acts. It is most commonly given as: $F = ma$

F = acting force $\qquad\qquad$ m = mass of body

a = acceleration

In terms of skating, when you are trying to move yourself, the more the body weight can be put into the push (along with the power from the straightening pushing leg) the greater the force and resulting acceleration. Conversely when you are stopping the more you can use the body weight in the stop the greater the force against the ice and the quicker you can stop. Finally the greater the acceleration the more force it will take to effect a stop.

Third Law—For every force which acts on a body (the action force), there is an equal and opposite force (reaction force) which acts on some other body.

In terms of skating, when you push against the ice with the edge of the blade the ice pushes back on the blade with an equal and opposite force which has the effect of moving you since your mass is relatively small compared to that of the ice.

TWO-FOOTED SKATING—FORWARD AND BACKWARD

It is obviously easier to balance on two skates than on only one. Skaters can take advantage of this fact and learn much about fundamentals of moving on ice by spending some time on this type of skating. Use it to learn 1) how to use the edges of your blades to move yourself forward or backward 2) how to use your legs to get a strong thrust against the ice with the edge of your blade 3) how to lean and balance on curves 4) where to balance on blades for forward and backward skating.

Balance Experiment

Assume the KEY POSTURE, (Fig. 6.1) turn the hips, legs and feet about 60° first to the right and then to the left, in a rhythmic alternating motion. Keep feet about 10–12 inches apart on slight inside edges. Results? Try to use this same motion to move yourself forward. Now use the same motion to move yourself backward. Can you perform the same motion and remain in one place? If you were able to succeed in going forward, backward and staying in place all with the same motion you can draw some conclusions about balance. If the weight is centered slightly behind the midpoint of the blade (i.e., more weight on the heel than ball of foot) the motion will move you forward. If the weight is centered slightly in front of the midpoint of the blade (more weight on ball of foot than heel) the motion will move you backward. If weight is over the center point of blades (equal weight over ball of foot and heel) you will stay in one place. *It is generally true that for all types of forward skating the balance should be centered slightly behind the center point of the blade; and for all types of backward skating the balance should be centered slightly in front of the center point of the blade.* The distance between these two balance points will vary with the type of blade. It will be larger for the figure blade than for the hockey blade, and will vary from one make of blade to another. Nevertheless, for all blades, you will skate toward the back of the blade for forward skating and toward the front of the blade for backward skating.

Double Sculling—Forward

Done entirely on the inside edges of both blades.

a

1. Start in KEY POSTURE with feet parallel and close, knees bent and forward.

2. Turn toes out and move feet apart pressing evenly on the inside edges of both blades, knees straighten slightly but do not stiffen . . . keep weight *just behind center point of blades.*

b

3. Turn toes in (stay on inside edges) and start bringing feet back to a parallel position. *Increase knee bend as feet come back together.*

c

4. Repeat from 1.

Be sure to take enough inside edge to grip the ice . . . if your ankles are up too straight and the edges are too shallow they will slip and you will not be able to exert any pressure against the ice. The farther apart your feet go the longer and harder you can push, and the faster you will go. This is an excellent exercise for developing leg power and inside edge thrust.

Double Sculling—Backward

1. Start in KEY POSTURE with feet parallel and close, knees bent.

2. Turn heels out and move feet apart pressing evenly with the inside edges of both blades—*keep weight in front of center point of blade.*

3. Turn heels in (be sure to stay on inside edges) and pull feet back to parallel position . . . increase knee bend as feet come together.
4. Repeat from 1.

There is definitely more of a feeling of push and pull to backward sculling. The push is felt as your feet go apart. The pull comes as you bring your feet together. Be sure that both feet stay on inside edges and that you press evenly with both edges.

35

Single Sculling—Forward and Backward

One foot makes a continuous out-in sculling motion on the inside edge
. . . the other foot simply rides on the flat of the blade.

1. Start in KEY POSTURE with feet parallel, knees bent, one foot on the flat of the blade and the other on an inside edge.

2. Turn toe (heel) of foot on inside edge out. Press it out to the side with a sculling motion using the inside edge and straighten the knee slightly. Bend knee of other leg and let weight shift to that side.

**Forward
single sculling**

3. Bring pushing foot back to a position parallel to the other foot. Increase knee bend as feet come together.

4. Repeat from 1.

   Note that all the pushing is done by one foot. This should take you across the ice in a straight line. This is a good exercise for a weak pushing leg. Keep pushing foot in front of you for backward single sculling, and *keep weight forward in front of center point of blade.*

**Backward
single sculling**

Alternate Sculling—Forward and Backward

Do a single scull on one foot then follow by a single scull on the opposite foot. Alternate sculling contains the whole sequence of movements used in stroking. For this reason it is very helpful to work diligently on this exercise until you can get a good powerful thrust from the pushing leg and a really deep knee bend in (and therefore weight shift to) the other leg.

For backward alternate sculling

1. Single scull first on one side then the other.
2. Keep pushing foot slightly in front so that you feel that you are pushing the ice away from in front of you.
3. Keep weight centered over a point slightly in front of center of blade.

Zig-Zag—Forward

The action is the same as for alternate sculling, but the non-pushing foot is on an outside edge instead of on the flat of the blade so the pattern is one of curves rather than straight. Arms and shoulders are rotated into the direction of the curve. This is a good exercise for getting the feeling of changing lean from one curve to another.

Zig-Zag—Backward

1. non-pushing foot on outside edge
2. arms and shoulders rotated into curve
3. head should look into curve
4. balance should be maintained slightly in front of center of blades
5. pushing foot is slightly in front

Scooter Forward

The pattern for this exercise is circular. Turn the upper body to the right. With right skate riding on the outside edge, pump with the inside edge of the left skate in a forward sculling motion as in single sculling. Lean right into the curve. Repeat in the opposite direction to the left. The scooter is excellent for learning to lean into the curve and for strengthening your outside edge.

Scooter Backward

Turn upper body toward the right and look back to the right (inside of the curve). Use the left inside edge in a backward sculling motion to pump around the circle. Keep the right foot riding on an outside edge. The pushing foot should stay slightly forward so that you feel that you are pushing the ice away from in front of you. Lean in to the right. Repeat in the opposite direction.

14.1. Forward   14.2. Backward

Figure 14. Scooters.

*   *   *   *   *

The two-footed exercises presented here are useful when you first learn to skate. But more than that, some of them will continue to be useful. Alternate sculling is used by many advanced skaters as a warm-up when they first go on the ice to loosen up the leg muscles and knees. Scooters are very helpful when you are learning crossovers and edges. In general, whatever time you spend on these exercises will be well spent, as you will find yourself rewarded with increased control of balance and power in all of your skating.

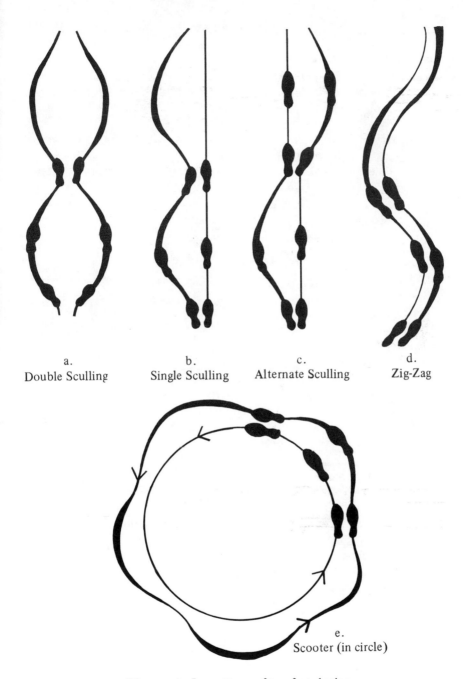

a.	b.	c.	d.
Double Sculling	Single Sculling	Alternate Sculling	Zig-Zag

e.
Scooter (in circle)

Diagram A. Ice patterns of two foot skating.

BALANCE TESTS

Beginner Test

1. Assume KEY POSTURE
2. Stand still on both feet with feet 10 to 12 inches apart. Bend knees to cover toes—then rise to straight knees—repeat, *without allowing feet to move.* _____
3. Move forward with any method of two-foot skating—*keep knees over toes and both feet on the ice.* _____
4. Glide in straight line on two feet on flats of blades knees over toes—*ankles must be held up straight.* _____
5. Glide in straight line forward on the right foot (on flat of blade) for a distance equal to 3 times your height. _____
6. Same as in 4—only on the left foot. _____

Intermediate Test

1. Assume KEY POSTURE
2. Glide on two feet forward on a curve to the left (counterclockwise) _____
   Body leans to the left (into curve) _____
   Knees over toes _____
   Left foot on outside edge _____
3. Glide on two feet forward on a curve to the right (clockwise) _____
   Body leans to right_____knees over toes _____
   Right foot on outside edge _____
4. Glide on the right foot forward in a straight line for 40 feet or more _____
   Skating knee over toe _____
   Foot that is off the ice carried to the side and back at 45° as in stroking _____
5. Glide on the left foot forward in a straight line for 40 feet or more _____
   Skating knee over toe_____Foot that is off the ice carried to the side and back at 45° as in stroking _____
   Back straight . . . shoulders over hips _____
6. Move backward with any method of two-foot skating _____
   Knees over toes _____
7. Glide in a straight line backward on two feet at least half way across ice _____
   Knees over toes _____

TWO FOOTED SKATING TESTS

Beginner Test

1. Double sculling—forward across the ice—knees over
   toes _____
   Even pressure on both inside edges _____
   Upper body maintains steady balance _____
2. Double sculling—backward across the ice—knees
   over toes _____
   Even pressure on both inside edges _____
   Upper body maintains steady balance _____
3. One foot sculling—forward across the ice _____
   a. Right foot pushing____left foot on flat of blade____left knee
   well bent _____
   b. Left foot pushing____right foot on flat of blade____right knee
   well bent _____

Intermediate Test

1. Alternate sculling—forward across the ice _____
   Even pushes with each foot____, good bend at knee in leg that is
   not pushing _____
2. One foot sculling—backward _____
   a. Right foot pushing____, push made slightly in front of left foot
   , left foot on flat of blade _____
   b. Left foot pushing____, push made slightly in front of right foot
   , right foot on flat of blade _____
3. Zigzag—forward across the ice—knees over toes _____
   Serpentine pattern____, body leans into curve____feet on opposite edges _____
4. Alternate sculling—backward across ice—knees over
   toes _____
   Even pushes with each foot _____
5. Forward scooter—counterclockwise _____
   Upper body turned into curve from waist (right arm in front, left
   arm in back) _____
   Left foot on outside edge____right foot pushing to *side* on inside
   edge—no picks _____
   Body leans to left____left knee bends during each
   push _____

6. Forward scooter—clockwise _____
   Upper body turned into curve from waist (left arm in front, right arm in back) _____
   Right foot on outside edge_____left foot pushing to *side* on inside edge—no picks _____
   Body leans to right_____right knee bends during each push _____

Advanced Test

1. Alternate sculling with power push across ice _____
   Touch ice with hand on every push (see chapter VI—power stroking)
   Nonpushing leg bends very deeply at knee _____
2. Zigzag—backward across ice
   Serpentine pattern_____body leans into curve_____feet on opposite edges _____
3. Backward scooter—counterclockwise _____
   Upper body turned in to curve from waist (left arm in front right arm in back)_____head looks in over right shoulder _____
   Right foot on outside edge_____left foot pushing on inside edge slightly in front of right foot _____
   Body leans to right_____right knee bends during push _____
4. Backward scooter—clockwise _____
   Upper body turned into curve from waist (right arm in front, left arm in back)_____head looks in over left shoulder _____
   Left foot on outside edge_____right foot pushing on inside edge slightly in front of left foot _____
   Body leans to left_____left knee bends during push _____
5. Forward scooters with power push—touch ice with inside hand on every push—bend inside knee deeply
   Counterclockwise . . . touch ice with left hand _____
   Clockwise . . . touch ice with right hand _____

Chapter V

Stroking Fundamentals

Good powerful smooth stroking requires three things as follows: 1) correct balance, 2) an efficient mechanism for obtaining power, 3) lots of practice. The first two are provided by the action of the knees in combination with the KEY POSTURE. The straightening of the pushing leg provides power in the thrust from the edge of the blade. The bending of the other leg in combination with the forward bend of the lower leg at the ankle provides the correct balance by lowering the center of gravity of the skater and bringing the weight over the center of the skate. In all types of stroking (forward, backward and crossovers) the knees are alternately bending and straightening as the weight shifts from foot to foot. THE PUSH ITSELF IS ALWAYS MADE FROM THE EDGE OF THE BLADE—NEVER, FROM THE TOE PICKS—THIS IS A FUNDAMENTAL REQUISITE OF GOOD TECHNIQUE. We can think of all stroking as having three phases: 1) the push, 2) the glide, 3) the recovery.

15.1. Push   15.2. Glide   15.3. Recovery

Figure 15. Forward stroking.

FORWARD STROKING

Start the push in the KEY POSTURE with the feet close together and the knees well bent. Push to the side with the inside edge of the blade which is angled at about 45° to the other foot. During the push straighten the pushing leg completely for maximum thrust. The transfer of weight occurs during the push. When it is completed at the end of the push, lift the pushing foot from the ice being careful to lift the whole blade at once in a position that is parallel to the ice. This is particularly important for the figure skater in order to prevent catching the 'picks' in an ugly toe push. After it is lifted from the ice the pushing foot is termed the free foot and the support foot is called the skating foot.

The glide position depends upon the style of skating (Fig. 16). For figure skating the glide begins on a well bent skating knee with the free leg extended at an angle of approximately 45° out and back. The free toe is pointed down and back. The free arm is extended forward; the skating arm is held extended out to the side. The head is erect; the back is straight but inclined slightly forward from the hips bringing the head over the skating foot. The hips face directly forward at all times when the skater is stroking. Any lateral turning of the pelvis is disastrous to good stroking. During the glide there may be a slight rise or straightening of the skating knee. The glide is done on a very slight inside edge.

The recovery occurs at the end of the glide when the skater is getting ready to push again. The feet are brought close together, there is a deepening of the knee bend in the skating leg and a corresponding deepening of the inside edge (this is really the beginning of the new push) and finally the body begins to lean toward the side of the free foot in anticipation of placing it on the ice. (Fig. 15.3)

In good stroking these three phases blend into a rhythmic continuously flowing cycle of movement that is beautiful to watch.

Differences in Styles of Forward Stroking

While the basic elements having to do with balance and power are the same for all types of skating, there are some significant points of difference in style between speed, hockey and figure skaters. These differences appear in the carriage or posture of the trunk of the body, the position of the pushing leg after the thrust, and the use of the arms. (Fig. 16).

The posture of the speed skater is such that the trunk of the body is inclined forward to an almost horizontal position. This posture is necessary in order to reduce the factor of wind resistance* and it is an advantage because of the lowered center of gravity; it is possible because the speed skating blade has very little curvature and extends well beyond the toe of the boot.

*Speed skating races are held outside usually.

Figure 16. Styles of stroking.

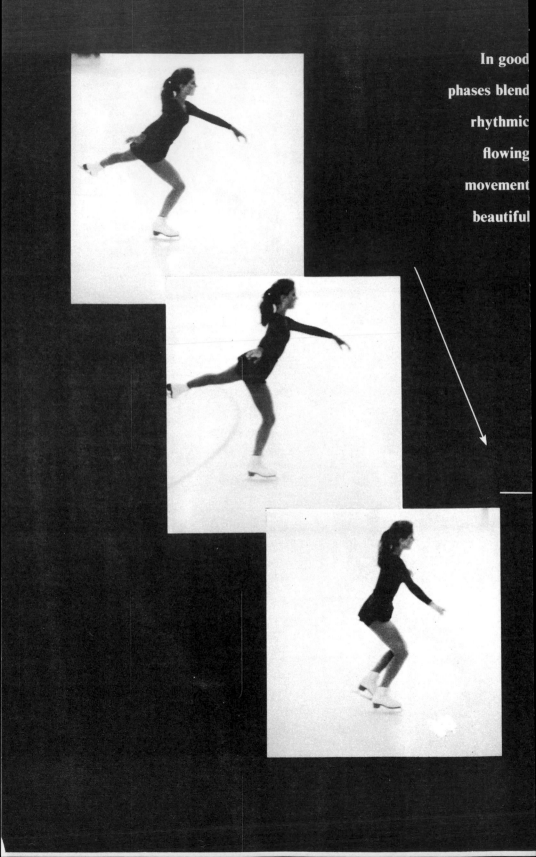

In good

phases blend

rhythmic

flowing

movement

beautiful

stroking all
into a
continuously
cycle of
that is
to watch!

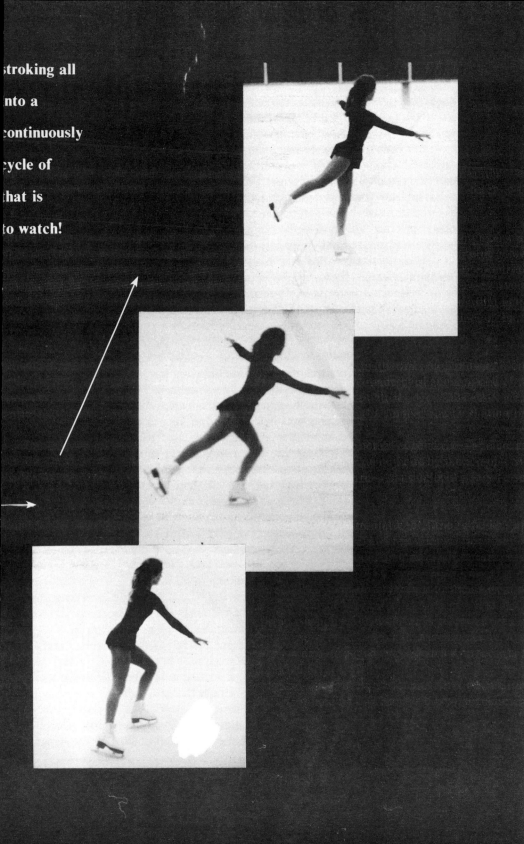

Figure skaters and hockey skaters incline the trunk only slightly forward, generally at the push offs—during acceleration. The angle of inclination varies from 15° to 40°, but should not exceed this or efficiency will be reduced, and in the case of the figure skater, too bent a position will spoil the body line and detract from the aesthetic appearance of the skater.

Both the speed skater and hockey player want to get maximum speed with a minimum of energy expenditure, therefore, after they have straightened the pushing leg in the thrust for power they let it relax and bend immediately, carrying it in a comfortable position throughout the glide in order to conserve energy. The figure skater by contrast, is willing to expend extra energy in order to maintain the straight extended free leg during the glide because it provides a more pleasing body line and adds elegance to the style.

Speed skaters use the arms in a swinging motion to aid in acquiring and maintaining speed. Hockey players must use the arms for stick handling, and figure skaters use the arms in ways that complete the body line and/or aid in the balance of particular skills. For all styles of skating the head should be held erect.

Improving Your Forward Stroking

Practice forward stroking every time that you skate, always working to increase your power and speed and to perfect your form. Have someone check you periodically against the stroking test at the end of this chapter.

To help in developing your balance and position in the glide portion of the stroke it is helpful to practice gliding on one foot for as long as you can. Take three strokes to get started, glide momentarily on two feet to be sure that you are going straight and that knees are bent, then shift all of your weight to one foot keeping the skating knee bent and the other foot close to the ice beside the skating foot. Try to hold your balance the rest of the way across the ice. Practice this first on one foot then the other. Be sure to hold the ankle up straight so that you are gliding straight forward on the "flat" of the blade, knee over toe and trunk erect. After you have succeeded in gliding on one foot with the feet close, try moving the free foot back and slightly to the side (at about 45°) so you are gliding in the stroking position.

Once you have developed your stroking balance you can turn your attention toward increasing your power and efficiency. As mentioned earlier the power comes from the straightening of the pushing leg as it thrusts the blade against the ice, so make sure that you form the habits of: 1) starting every stroke with both knees bent and the feet close together, 2) straightening the pushing leg completely on each push, and 3) deepening the inside edge and knee bend at the end of the recovery to initiate the new push.

As you continue to work on your stroking you will find yourself developing your own rhythm of movement, especailly if you have music accompanying your skating. Once you have formed the habit of starting the stroke on a well bent knee you can add a rise on the knee during the glide and a return to the bend at the end of the glide just before the new push. This will add a down-up-down action to the stroke that gives it a pleasant rhythmic lilt.

BACKWARD STROKING

Backward stroking like forward stroking is a matter of pushing from one foot to the other while moving oneself along the line of travel. It is a skill used mostly by figure skaters.

The push is started with the feet very close together. The heel of the pushing foot is aimed out to the side in a sculling motion. Pressure is exerted downward against the ice with the whole inside edge of the blade. The pushing foot is kept slightly forward of the other foot as in backward single sculling. The weight remains slightly forward of the center of the blade and shifts from the pushing foot to the other foot in the push. (Fig. 17.1). At the end of the push the pushing leg is fully extended and the foot is lifted from the ice and carried in front during the glide. (Fig. 17.2).

In the glide position the skating knee should be well bent with the weight centered just in front of the center point of the blade. The free leg is carried extended in front with the free foot close to the ice and with the toe pointed down. The arms are carried extended to the sides with the hands at waist height and slightly forward of the body.

In the recovery phase the feet and legs are brought close together, knee-bend of the skating leg is increased and the body lean changes toward the new skating foot as the push begins from a inside edge. (Fig. 17.3)

17.1. Push   17.2. Glide   17.3. Recovery

Figure 17. Backward stroking.

Getting Started on Backward Stroking

Begin* with alternate sculling backward (see Chap. IV) and practice bringing the feet together after each push during the glide, so that you become accustomed to a narrower support base. When you can do this easily start lifting the pushing foot during the glide. Keep this foot close to the ice and forward of your skating foot. Glide on the other foot with weight just in front of the center of the blade. Eventually eliminate the two foot glide and lift the pushing leg at the end of the push and extend it forward in the glide. The glide may be done on slight inside or outside edges but the push is always from the inside edge.

Gliding backward on one foot across the ice on the flat of blade will help you develop the balance you need in backward stroking. This can be done by starting with your two-footed backward skating for a few pushes then gliding on two feet close together and finally shifting all the weight to one foot and lifting the other forward as you glide as far as you can in a straight line. Be sure to keep the supporting knee flexed in the glide and the trunk and head erect. If you find yourself traveling on a curve check to see if you are letting the ankle fall in or out, or if you are turning the shoulders. The ankle should be held straight up so that your weight is right on top of the blade with both edges touching, and the shoulders should be facing forward at right angles to the direction of travel.

If you have not done any backward stroking before, you can expect to take quite some time before you really feel balanced and comfortable doing it. Practice and be patient. A partner who will skate forward in front of you and provide support in the early learning stages can be very helpful.

CROSSOVERS

The forward and backward stroking just described is known as 'open' stroking and its pattern is more or less a straight line. A different kind of stroking is used when travelling on curves or turning. This kind of stroking involves a crossing of the feet and a push from the outside edge of the skate that is in back. Crossover strokes alternate with open strokes when the skater is travelling on a curve. During the open stroke the foot that isn't pushing travels on an outside edge as the body leans into the curve so this stroke is really like a scooter push (see Chap. IV.). Crossovers are power strokes that provide speed on curves.

*Do not begin backward stroking until you can skate with good balance and speed backward on two feet.

18.1.

18.2.

18.3.

18.1. Open stroke.
18.2. Beginning of crossover—right foot placed ahead, weight begins to shift to right foot.
18.3. Left foot crosses behind. Left leg begins to straighten in push—crossed glide position.

18.4.

18.5.

18.4. Right leg bends to take weight as left leg pushes—deep crossed-glide position.
18.5. At end of push left foot is lifted from ice (note blade is parallel to ice).

Figure 18. Forward crossovers.

51

19.1. Push

19.2. Glide

19.3. Recovery

Figure 19.

Getting Started on Forward Crossovers
Know Your Edges!

Since crossovers are always done on curves it is first of all necessary for you to get the feeling of skating on a curve. This means skating on edges and leaning in to the curve. WHENEVER YOU TRAVEL ON A CURVE THE FEET WILL BE ON OPPOSITE EDGES. *The outside foot (The one farthest from the center of the circle) will always travel on an inside edge and the inside foot (the one closest to the center of the circle) will travel on an outside edge. This is always true whether you are moving backward or forward on one foot or two feet.*

Forward Crossovers

The forward crossover stroke is always initiated at the end of the open stroke after the push is completed (Fig. 18.1) by bringing the foot that is on the outside of the curve (i.e. the right foot if moving in a counterclockwise direction) forward and placing it on the ice on an inside edge in front of the other foot (Fig. 18.2). The body weight begins to shift to the front foot as the knee bends. At the same time the back foot crosses to the outside of the curve and as the leg straightens, and pushes with the outside edge of the blade against the ice. At the end of this push the foot in back is lifted from the ice, and brought back around the other foot to the inside ready to be placed beside it for the next open stroke.

Crossover strokes can be considered to have the same three phases as open strokes i.e. push, glide, recovery.

The push is begun as the outside leg moves forward and the inside foot (becoming the back foot) presses with the outside edge to the outside of the curve as this leg straightens. The weight shifts in the push from the back foot to the front foot which is placed on the inside edge. As in all stroking power comes from edge pressure and the straightening of the pushing leg.

At the end of the thrust when the pushing leg is completely extended and the weight has shifted to the front foot, the pushing foot is lifted from the ice. (Fig. 19.2). If the skater is wearing figure skates he must be careful to hold the back leg straight and the heel of the blade down until the whole blade is lifted at once in such a way that it is parallel to the ice. If the back leg bends, the heel comes up first and the push will be cut off prematurely by the picks going into the ice forcing the skater to transfer all the weight to the front foot in a sharp, jerky motion that has lost most of the power of the push.

The glide is usually cut short in a crossover stroke, but it should be held at least momentarily. The position should be that taken when the pushing foot leaves the ice with the back leg fully extended to the outside of the curve and crossed behind the front leg. (Fig. 18.5).

During the recovery to the new push position it is necessary to return the back foot to the inside of the curve and place it next to the other foot ready for the open stroke. The knee must bend in order for this to be accomplished. The open stroke will be made with the outside* foot thrusting to the side to the outside of the curve with the inner* edge of the blade pushing against the ice as weight transfers to the inside foot (which will be gliding on an outside edge) (Fig. 18.1). At the end of the open stroke the outside foot will again be brought ahead and placed in front of the inside foot in order to begin the next crossover stroke.

*The terms outside and inside when designating one foot or the other refer to their position relative to the center of the curve or circle on which the skater is traveling; when the same terms are applied to edges the reference is to the foot itself—inside edge being the one nearest the instep side of foot etc.

Body Position

For all crossovers the upper body is turned in toward the center of the curve from the waist. This brings the arms, which are extended, into a position parallel to the curve with the outside arm in front of the body and the inside arm behind the body.

Airplane Glides (for learning to lean on curves and to practice the body position for crossovers)

Skate forward to gain some speed then extend arms out to sides like wings, turn upper body to the left and with feet apart glide on a curve to the left. Bend the inside (left) knee and straighten the outside (right) one and lean body and blades to the left. Keeping the feet apart will give you a broad base of support and allow you to take a good lean and edges. Repeat on curve to right.

Scooter Drill (for the open push and the feeling of lean in to the circle)

With the left foot on the outside edge and with the upper body turned to the left, push to the side with the inside edge of the right skate. Lift the right skate at the end of the push (with the blade parallel to the ice so there is no toe push) and bring it back beside the left skate to repeat the push. Continue around the circle doing these open scooter pushes. Be sure to push *to the side from the edge of the blade and not backward from the toe.* Maintain a good outside edge on the other foot and a good lean into the circle. Repeat in the opposite direction.

Crossed-Foot Glide

When you can pump with ease around a circle doing the scooter, you should go on to do a crossed foot glide as follows: start in a counterclockwise direction with a scooter motion to gain some speed, (upper body turned into curve, right arm leading, left arm in back). Next bring the right foot forward and place it on the ice on the curve in front of the left foot—keep lean of body into center. At this point the weight is mainly on the left foot. Bend right knee and start shifting weight to it; at the same time allow the left foot to move across behind the right foot to the outside of the curve—straighten left leg. Try to glide in this crossed position and gradually shift more and more weight to the deeply bent right knee. Practice gliding in this crossed glide position both in the counterclockwise and clockwise direction. (Fig. 18.3,4)

Next, start with three scooter pushes on a circle going counterclockwise, shoulders turned into curve. At the end of the third push bring the right foot ahead (don't step over left foot to cross—just step ahead) keeping it close to the ice and place it on the ice in front of left foot, continue into the crossed glide position and transfer weight entirely to the right foot so that you can lift left foot (which is behind) completely off the ice with left leg straight. Hold this position momentarily and glide on the right inside forward edge. At the end of the glide bring the left foot back inside of the curve and place it next to the right foot (bend left knee to do this) and repeat the three scooter pushes and crossed glide. As you continue to practice this, reduce the number of scooter pushes between the crossed glides to two and then to one. When you reach this point you are essentially doing a series of alternate open and crossover strokes. Keep working to gain a feeling of balance on the glides—on the outside edge for the left foot and inside edge for the right foot. As your confidence and balance improve you can start to push harder on the open stroke (don't use picks if you're on figure blades), but for a while don't push on the crossover stroke just transfer the weight smoothly and gradually and make sure the left foot is traveling out of the curve on the outside edge as it crosses behind right foot. Eventually you will want to thrust with this outside edge for power,* but first you have to be sure that you are getting on the edge. If you are on figure skates, when you lift the back foot from the ice you must be careful to lift the whole blade at once, and not the heel first leaving the pick in the ice. Keep the back leg straight until that foot is completely off the ice, then bend it in the air to bring it back around to the inside of the other leg.

The forward crossover strokes should be learned and practiced in both a clockwise and counterclockwise direction. Use the same series of steps to work on the clockwise direction.

Because skating on a curve or a circle involves two different edges and two different strokes (i.e., open scooter and crossed) it is necessary to match the kneebend in the legs when changing feet. If the knee bends more on the open stroke than the crossover or vice versa the pushes will be uneven and likewise the resulting power. For maximum efficiency and a smooth appearance the knees must bend equally on both strokes and the thrust must be made with the same speed from the inside and outside edges. When this occurs the skater appears to move effortlessly with great speed over the ice.

Backward Crossovers

The main differences from the forward crossovers are as follows: 1) *The outside foot on the curve is never lifted from the ice.* After the open push it slides across on the ice on the inner edge of the blade in front of the other foot as the weight is transferred to it. 2) *The head is turned to look behind the skater along the inside of the curve.* 3) *The point of balance is slightly in front of the center of the blades.*

*See Power Stroking—Chap. VII

55

| 20.1. Push | 20.2. Glide |

Figure 20. Back crossover.

The push begins as the outside foot is being drawn across in front of the other foot on the inside edge. The back foot is pushing across and out of the curve as it thrusts from the outside edge. The weight shifts from the back foot to the front foot during the push. As in other strokes the pushing leg extends completely in the thrust and is then lifted from the ice with the blade parallel to the ice to prevent toe pushing (Fig. 20.1). Only after the foot is lifted from the ice is the pushing leg bent to bring the foot back around to the inside of the curve during the recovery for the next push. Any attempt to take the foot back and off the ice at the same time results in toe scratching. Holding the glide position (Fig. 20.2) with the back leg extended momentarily not only creates a good 'line', but guards against toe pushing.

Getting Started on Backward Crossovers

Body Position

As in the forward crossovers the upper body is turned in from the waist toward the center of the curve. The arms are extended along the line of the curve with the outside arm in front and the inside arm in back of the skater.

Airplane Glides (for learning the lean, edges, and body position)

Skate backward to gain some speed, arms extended, turn upper body to the right, with the head looking back to the right, and glide backwards on a curve to the right. The feet should be about 10–12 inches apart on the correct edges with the outside foot slightly forward of the other foot. The body leans into the curve.

Backward Scooter Drill (for the open push and feeling of lean on the edges)

With the right foot on the outside edge and with the upper body turned to the right, push to the side with the inside edge of the left blade in a backward sculling motion. Look to the right behind you as you pump around in a circle to the right. Keep the pumping foot (left) slightly in front of the other foot so you feel that you are pushing the ice away in front of you. Lean to the right (in to the curve) over a well bent right knee. Do not lift the pushing foot from the ice at any time. Maintain a good outside edge on the other foot and a good lean into the circle. Repeat in the opposite direction.

Crossed-Foot Glide

When you can pump with ease around the circle with the backward scooter, go on to do a crossed foot glide. After you have gained some speed using the scooter, glide for a moment while you move your outside foot (on the ice) forward in front of the other foot. Continue to move the front foot across the path of the other foot (by aiming the heel in toward the center of the curve) until it is on the inside of the curve and the feet are crossed and parallel. Keep the hips square to the line of the curve and the head looking back and inside the curve. The body weight shifts from the inside foot to the one coming across in front; so in the glide it is on the front foot. Practice in both directions.

As you practice the crossed foot glides gradually start shifting more and more weight to the front foot until you can lift the back foot off the ice and balance on the inside back edge with the back leg extended to the outside of the curve. This is the position you will have during the glide of the crossover stroke. In order to be ready for the next push it is necessary to return the back foot to the inside of the curve and position it next to the other foot during the recovery period of the stroke. (Note—this is the only point during the back crossover that you are balanced on just one foot.)

21.2. Crossover

21.1. Open push

Figure 21. Back crossover positions. Note good body lean.

Try skating around a circle now with three scooter pushes and then a crossover and repeat. Be sure to keep the back straight so the hips are under shoulders; make the legs do the work and keep hips aligned square to the line of the circle. As you practice reduce the number of scooter pushes between crossovers until you are alternately skating a crossover then an open stroke continuously around the curve. In the beginning do not try for speed, but rather for developing good balance on both feet so that you are not falling from one stroke to another.

FORWARD STROKING TEST

Key Posture (held throughout push, glide and recovery)

Back is straight   _____

Slight forward bend at hips (less than 40°)   _____

Head erect   _____

Eyes looking out not down   _____

Hands in front of line of shoulders (if arms held out to sides)   _____

Push

Feet close together   _____

Both knees bent and forward to cover toes   _____

Side push from inside edge (no picks)   _____

Pushing leg straightens completely in thrust   _____

Skating leg increases kneebend at end of push   _____

Glide—Figure Skater

Begins on deeply bent skating knee   _____
Can rise to straighten knee during glide and resume bend at end of glide

Free leg carried extended and straight at 45° throughout glide   _____

Glide—Hockey Skater

Begins on deeply bent skating knee may or may not rise on skating knee during glide   _____
Pushing leg relaxes and bends after thrust and is carried in back during glide   _____

Recovery

Skating kneebend increases   _____

Deepened inner edge—Body begins to lean in direction of new stroke   _____

Feet brought close—with both knees bent   _____

Stroke Length

Equal at least to height of skater   _____

Equal on both feet   _____

Clean weight transfer (no two-footed skating between pushes)   _____

General

Smooth continuous action of knees   _____

Good flow in all phases of stroke   _____

CROSSOVER TESTS

Forward Crossover—Counterclockwise

1. *Forward Scooter*—Counterclockwise
   Upper body turned into curve from waist (right arm in front, left arm in back)   _____
   Left foot on outside edge—right foot pushing to *side* on inside edge—no picks   _____
   Body leans to left—left knee bends during each push   _____
2. *Crossed-foot glide* (on two feet) counterclockwise forward
   Right foot in front on good inside edge   _____
   Right knee well bent and carrying most of the weight   _____
   Left foot crossed in back on good outside edge   _____
   Left leg is straight   _____
   Upper body turned into curve from waist   _____
   Right arm in front—left arm in back   _____
   Hold for at least 15 feet   _____
3. *Skate around in a circle, forward, counterclockwise, with alternate open and crossover strokes*
   Upper body turned into curve   _____
   Good side push from inside edge on open strokes
   (no picks)   _____
   Stepping ahead on crossover (not over other foot)   _____
   Back foot crossing out at least 6 inches   _____
   No picks as back foot leaves ice   _____

Forward Crossover—Clockwise

1. *Forward scooter*—Clockwise
   Upper body turned into curve from waist (left arm in front, right arm in back)   _____
   Right foot on outside edge—left foot pushing to *side* on inside edge—no picks   _____
   Body leans to right—right knee bends during each push   _____
2. *Crossed-foot glide* (on two feet) clockwise-forward
   Left foot in front on good inside edge   _____
   Left knee well bent and carrying most of the weight   _____
   Right foot crossed in back on good outside edge   _____
   Right leg straight   _____
   Upper body turned into curve from waist   _____
   Left arm in front—right arm in back   _____
   Hold glide for at least 15 feet   _____

61

3. *Skate around in a circle, forward clockwise, with alternate open and crossover strokes*
   Upper body turned into curve _____
   Good side push from inside edge on open strokes
   (no picks) _____
   Stepping ahead on crossover (not over other foot) _____
   Back foot crossing out at least 6 inches _____
   No picks as back foot leaves ice _____

Backward Crossover—Clockwise

1. *Backward scooter*—clockwise
   Upper body turned into curve from waist (right arm in front, left arm in back) _____
   Head looks in over left shoulder _____
   Left foot on outside edge _____
   Right foot pushing from inside edge _____
   Right foot slightly in front of left _____
   Body leans to left _____
   Left knee well bent during push _____
2. *Crossed foot glide*—backward—clockwise
   Right foot is crossed in front on good inside edge _____
   Right knee is well bent and carrying most of weight _____
   Left foot is crossed behind on good outside edge _____
   Left foot is at least 1 foot outside of right foot _____
   Left leg is completely straight _____
   Upper body is turned into curve _____
   Head looks in over left shoulder _____
3. *Backward Crossovers—in a circle*—clockwise
   (Skate alternately on open and cross stroke—keep right foot on ice throughout)
   Upper body turned into curve _____
   Shoulders level _____
   Head looking back over left shoulder _____
   Good push from inside edge on open stroke (no picks) _____
   Good push from outside edge on crossed stroke (no picks) _____
   Back foot crossing out at least 6 inches _____

Backward Crossover—Counterclockwise

1. *Backward scooter*—counterclockwise

   Upper body turned in to curve from waist (left arm in front right arm in back)—head looks in over right shoulder _____

   Right foot on outside edge—left foot pushing on inside edge slightly in front of right foot _____

   Body leans to right—right knee bends during push _____

2. *Crossed foot glide*—backward on two feet—counterclockwise

   Left foot is in front on good inside edge _____

   Left knee well bent and carrying most of the weight _____

   Right foot crossed in back on good outside edge _____

   Right leg straight _____

   Upper body turned into curve—head looks over right shoulder _____

   Left arm in front—right arm in back _____

   Hold glide for at least 15 feet _____

3. *Backward crossovers—skate around in a circle backward with alternate open and crossover strokes (keep left foot on ice all of the time)*

   Upper body turned into curve—shoulders level _____

   Good push from inside edge on open stroke (no picks) _____

   Back foot crossing out at least 6 inches _____

   No picks as back foot leaves ice _____

Chapter VI

Stops and Turns

STOPPING

All stops involve a skidding action in which the edge of the blade skids along the ice and shaves or scrapes its surface. The orientation of the scraping foot or feet is usually at right angles to the direction of the travel. Learn the stops at low speeds then gradually build up more speed. Think of the stopping process as a gradual one involving a period of sliding or skidding before finally stopping.

The Snowplow Stop, (See Chap. III). Modified Hockey Stop and T-Stop are all good stops for beginners. People seem to differ as to which of these is easiest to learn. It is a good idea to try all three, then concentrate on the one that seems easiest to you until you can do it with speed and control; then go on to the other two. Do not attempt the advanced stops until you have mastered the simple stops.

Modified Hockey Stop

This stop involves a quarter of a turn by the body and a braking action or skid of the leading foot on an inside edge. At the end of the stop the feet are spaced apart and the body has rotated one quarter of a turn.

Full hockey stop.

Learning the full hockey stop by pulling in to barrier.

Full Hockey Stop

In the full hockey stop the feet are parallel and close together. The front foot is on the inside edge and the trailing foot is on an outside edge. The weight is distributed over both feet. The shoulders remain facing the direction of travel even when the hips and feet turn. There is a definite unweighting action that occurs when the feet are turned. This is accomplished by rising up slightly on the knees and shifting the weight to the front of the skates as the feet turn, then sinking back down on the knees as you slide and stop with weight concentrated over the balls of the feet. Stand about two feet away and face the barrier, feet together, knees bent. Reach out and put hands on barrier so that you can pull yourself into it. The timing should be as follows; down . . . at the start, up . . . as you start pulling and turn your feet, down again . . . as you slide on both edges into the barrier. It may be easier at first to put most of your weight on the leading foot and then gradually increase the amount on the back foot as you practice. Once you have the feeling of the slide on both edges, try the stop away from the barrier. Remember . . . down . . . up . . . down, and keep the weight on the balls of the feet as you slide.

The T-Stop

The feet are placed in a "T"* position with the instep of the back foot at the heel of the front foot. The slide or scrape is made with the outside edge of the back foot; the front foot is on the flat of the blade. Weight shifts from the front foot to the back foot.

To get the feeling of sliding on the outside edge . . . face the barrier, and place the feet in a "T" position (back foot pointing to barrier, front foot parallel to barrier), be sure back foot is on the outside edge. Both knees should be slightly bent . . . with most of the weight on the front foot. Now reach ahead with your hands on the barrier and pull yourself along.

*Some people have difficulty with this position . . . if this is the case it helps to think of forcing the knees apart to enable the feet to make the "T".

67

Learn the "T" stop first from standstill on two feet at the barrier. Begin with feet parallel to barrier and to each other. Place most of the weight on the foot farthest from the barrier and place the foot nearest to the barrier on a slight outside edge. Now draw (on the ice) the foot nearest the barrier around behind the heel of the other foot (by rotating the leg outward and aiming the heel toward the other foot) until the feet are in a "T" position. Be sure the back foot is still on the outside edge. Move the back foot (on the ice) back to the original parallel position. Do this a number of times and add a gradual weight shift to the back foot. Next, begin by gliding along the barrier on two feet, repeat the process just learned at standstill and as you assume the T-position shift the weight gently to the outside edge of the foot in back.

This method is the most suitable and safest for beginners who usually have difficulty balancing on one foot, because the entire preparation and stop is done with both feet on the ice. Later when you have mastered the stop from this preparation you may go on to doing the stop from a one foot glide.

Backward Stops

Like the modified forward hockey stop this back stop relies on the friction produced by the use of the inside edge shaving the ice to stop the motion. If you have already learned the forward stop, you will find this back stop very easy. You can use the same three step approach to get the feeling of the stop at the barrier.

Step 1. Face the barrier with knees bent. Slide the foot (preferably the same one that you use for the forward hockey stop) to the side scraping the ice with the inside edge. Keep a steady pressure on the sliding foot; keep weight over the balls of the feet.

Step 2. With your hands on the barrier, turn sideways to it with your sliding foot nearest it. Turn a quarter of a turn toward the barrier and slide foot as in step 1. Finish facing the barrier.

Step 3. Move backward along the barrier, (with sliding foot next to the barrier) turn, slide and stop. Finish facing the barrier.

Another backward stop that is used often in hockey is the one where the heels are together and the toes are turned out as both feet slide on inside edges and the body leans forward.

ADVANCED STOPS

One Foot Stops

The stops already discussed can easily be modified into a stop on one foot. For figure skaters the one foot stop has more style and elegance, and a good hockey player has to be able to stop on either foot and on either edge.

One Foot Stop . . . Inside Edge

Start with your hockey stop but gradually increase the knee bend and the amount of weight on the leading foot . . . until all of your weight is on that foot. Pulling into barrier as described for hockey stop using only the leading foot, is helpful in gaining the feeling of the slide. Be sure to keep your weight on the ball of the foot and keep the knee flexible.

One foot stop inside edge.

One Foot Stop . . . Outside Edge

If you modify your hockey stop to a one foot stop on the outside edge follow the same procedures as given above, except use the trailing or back foot. If you have a strong "T" stop, it may be easier for you to modify it into an outside one foot stop rather than the hockey stop. To do this . . . after you have started to slide . . . shift your weight entirely to the back foot and lift the front foot off of the ice.

One foot stop outside edge.

TURNS

As soon as you can move forward and backward on the ice it is useful to be able to turn around from one direction to the other. ALTHOUGH THERE ARE MANY DIFFERENT WAYS OF TURNING ON THE ICE, THEY ALL INVOLVE THE SAME BASIC MECHANISMS AS FOLLOWS:

1. Erect posture with shoulders and hips level to provide a firm central axis of rotation.
2. Rotation of the upper part of the body as preparation for the turn.
3. A weight shift on the blade or blades at the turn.
4. A counter rotation (called checking) of the upper part of the body after the turn.

If you can learn to incorporate these mechanisms into your turns in the beginning you will have good control of the simple turns and you will find it easy to proceed to the advanced turns.

Two-Foot Turns

Learn these turns at the barrier first while you experiment with the weight shift.

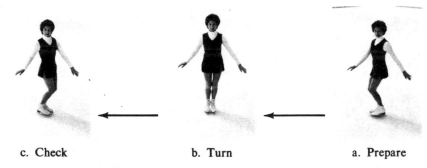

| c. Check | b. Turn | a. Prepare |

Forward turn on two feet: (a) upper body rotated to left (b) rise up on knees, shift weight to front of blades as feet turn (c) after turn keep upper body turned to right to hold checked position.

1. Rotate the upper body from the waist in the direction that you are going to turn. This will result in one arm being in front of you and one being in back.
2. Keep feet close together on the flat of the blades, knees slightly bent.
3. At turn rise up on knees and shift weight forward for forward turn or backward for backward turn.
4. Rotate feet and hips simultaneously with the weight shift (always turn toward the hand in back of you).
5. Check the turn by reversing the rotation in the upper body.

You can think of every turn as having three parts—the preparation, the turn itself, and the check.

After you have experimented at the barrier, move away and try the turn in a straight line at a slow speed. As your confidence increases so may your speed.

Two-foot turns can also be done on curves by skating on edges instead of flats. You will have to rotate the upper body into the curve during the preparation and check harder after the turn because of the extra rotational force from the edges. It is helpful to do these turns before going on to the three turns.

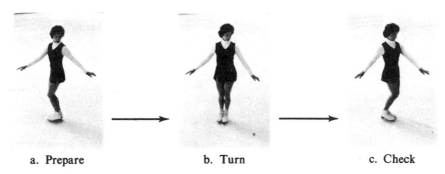

| a. Prepare | b. Turn | c. Check |

Backward turn on two feet: (a) upper body rotated to left—head must look in direction of travel (b) rise up on knees as weight shifts to heels of blades during turn (c) after turn keep upper body turned to right in checked position.

Forward Three Turns

It is possible to turn on one foot instead of two feet. The easiest and most common one-foot turn is the three turn, so called because the trace made on the ice looks like the numeral 3. Three turns can be done forward or backward from either edge. The direction of rotation is into the curve and the starting edge is opposite of the finishing edge but on the same curve. If you begin on an outside edge, after the turn you will be on an inside edge traveling on the same curve. Turns are named by the starting edge, and abbreviated by the initials standing for the words—i.e., Right Outside Forward Three (ROF).

The movement pattern for the three turns is the same as for the two-foot turns on a curve, but you must begin on one foot on an edge. For all forward three turns the free foot is held in back during the preparation for the turn. So your position before the turn is with the upper body rotated into the curve and the free foot extended in back. At the turn itself bring your free foot to the heel of your skating foot and shift your weight to the front of the blade as you turn your feet and hips. After the turn the free foot again extends in back and you check the turn with the arms and upper body as you ride out on the back edge.

71

One difference exists between the inside and outside forward three turns (other than edges) and that has to do with the checked position after the turn. For the outside forward threes the free hip and leg are held back in an open position to help check the turn. On the inside three this is not necessary the check being done with the upper body, arms and head.

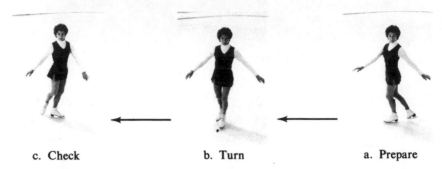

| c. Check | b. Turn | a. Prepare |

Left outside forward three turn: (a) upper body is turned to the left, hips square, free foot back (b) feet together as weight shifts to front of skate at turn (c) after turn shoulders, thorax, hips and free leg are kept turned to right.

Try the three turns at the barrier first for the weight shift and positions. Move away from the barrier, and if a partner is available, have him/her hold your inside hand as you skate a three turn on small curve. Do your first three turns alone on small curves, being sure to keep hips and shoulders level before and after turn.

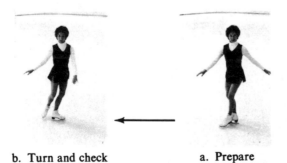

| b. Turn and check | a. Prepare |

Right inside forward Mohawk: (a) upper body and hips turned to left heel of free foot at instep of skating foot just before turn (b) after turn upper body, hips and free leg are kept turned to the right.

Inside Forward Mohawk

In addition to two-foot turns and one-foot turns there is another kind of turn that you can add to your skills. It involves stepping from one foot to the other and moving from one edge to another of the same kind—i.e., inside forward to inside back or outside forward to outside back. This type of turn is called a *Mohawk*.

The right inside forward Mohawk is done in a counterclockwise direction and involves the same movement pattern that you have learned with the two-foot turns and the three turns on that curve. The difference will be—(1) in the action of the feet before and during the turn and (2) in the action of the torso which moves as a unit—through these turns—i.e., the hips, thorax and shoulders move simultaneously into and out of the turn; whereas, in the one-foot turns, the upper torso rotates in advance of the rest of the body.

The RIF Mohawk begins on a RIF edge. To prepare for the turn rotate the entire torso into the curve and bring the heel of the free foot to the instep of the skating foot. (Be sure to keep posture erect—shoulders and hips level.) The skating knee should be slightly bent. Rise up on the skating knee as you turn the left foot and leg to the left and replace your right foot with the left one which is now facing backward on the LIB edge. After the turn check with the whole torso and free leg. The lift to a straight knee as you turn is very important in getting over the turn smoothly and cleanly. The most difficult thing is to get the timing of the quick turning of the free foot and leg synchronized with the weight shift. If the turning is too slow or the weight shift too early, the Mohawk will be scraped.

STOP TESTS

Beginner Test Demonstrate any one stop

    1. Snowplow stop
       Can take one stroke and stop with balance   _____
       Even pressure on both blades   _____
       Can skate across ice and stop (completely) with
       balance   _____
    2. Modified Hockey Stop
       Can take one stroke and stop and hold position for count of 3

       Knees bent____weight on balls of feet   _____
       Can see skid mark on ice from inside edge of front
       foot   _____
       Arms out to sides for balance   _____
       Can skate across ice and stop and hold position for count of 3

    3. T-Stop
       Can take one stroke and stop with balance   _____
       Back foot on outside edge____front foot on flat of
       blade   _____
       Feet at right angles—heel to instep in T position   _____
       Arms to side____both knees slightly bent   _____

Intermediate Test

    1. Full hockey stop
       Good slide on both edges____both knees bent   _____
       Weight on balls of feet   _____
       After stop can hold balanced position for count of 3   _____
    2. Any backward stop (not using picks)
       Can skate one stroke and stop with control   _____
       Can skate across ice backward and stop with control   _____

Advanced Test

    1. One foot stop . . . either foot, either edge   _____
    2. Hockey stop with speed . . . hold position for count
       of 3   _____
    3. Backward stop with speed . . . hold for count of 3   _____
    4. T-stop with speed . . . finish with control . . . no
       turning   _____

TURN TESTS

Beginner Test

   1. Forward turn on two feet to the right ⎯⎯⎯⎯
   Posture erect—shoulders and hips level ⎯⎯⎯⎯
   Upper body turned to the right before turn ⎯⎯⎯⎯
   Unweight skates at turn—(figure skates weight shifts to front of skates) ⎯⎯⎯⎯
   No loss of speed at turn ⎯⎯⎯⎯
   After turn rotation is checked by keeping upper body turned to the left momentarily ⎯⎯⎯⎯
   2. Forward turn on two feet to the left ⎯⎯⎯⎯
   Posture erect—shoulders and hips level ⎯⎯⎯⎯
   Upper body turned to the left before turn ⎯⎯⎯⎯
   Unweight skates at turn ⎯⎯⎯⎯
   No loss of speed at turn ⎯⎯⎯⎯
   After turn, rotation is checked by keeping upper body turned to right momentarily ⎯⎯⎯⎯

Intermediate Test

   1. Forward turn on two feet on curve—counterclockwise ⎯⎯⎯⎯
   2. Forward turn on two feet on curve—clockwise ⎯⎯⎯⎯
   3. Backward turn on two feet—straight line ⎯⎯⎯⎯
   4. One-foot turn forward in straight line ⎯⎯⎯⎯
   Free foot back before turn ⎯⎯⎯⎯
   Upper body rotates before turn ⎯⎯⎯⎯
   Feet together at turn ⎯⎯⎯⎯
   Weight shifts to front of skate at turn (on hockey skate—stay in middle of blade) ⎯⎯⎯⎯
   Free foot back after turn ⎯⎯⎯⎯
   Upper body, free leg and free hip check rotation after turn ⎯⎯⎯⎯

Advanced Test

   1. Left outside forward three turn ⎯⎯⎯⎯
   Good outside edge on left foot ⎯⎯⎯⎯
   Posture erect—hips and shoulders level ⎯⎯⎯⎯
   Upper body rotated to left to prepare for turn ⎯⎯⎯⎯
   Right foot back before turn ⎯⎯⎯⎯
   Feet close at turn ⎯⎯⎯⎯
   Weight shifts to front of skate in turn ⎯⎯⎯⎯
   After turn, weight on front of skate ⎯⎯⎯⎯
   Upper body, free leg and hip turned to right in checked position after turn ⎯⎯⎯⎯

2. Right inside forward three turn   _____
   Good inside edge on right foot   _____
   Posture erect—hips and shoulders level   _____
   Upper body rotated to left to prepare for turn _____
   Left foot back before turn   _____
   Feet close at turn   _____
   Weight shifts to front of skate at turn   _____
   After turn, weight on front of skate   _____
   Free foot back after turn   _____
   Check with upper body after turn   _____
3. Right inside forward Mohawk   _____
   Shoulders and hips rotated to left before turn _____
   Left heel at right instep at turn   _____
   Right knee straightens at turn   _____
   After turn weight on front of left skate   _____
   Free foot back after turn   _____
   Upper body, free hip and leg turned to right after
   turn   _____

Chapter VII

Power Skating and Conditioning

POWER SKATING

Open Stroking

Power in stroking—either forwards or backward—results from the straightening of the pushing leg as it thrusts the edge of the blade against the ice. It follows therefore, that the deeper the bend of the leg at the knee the greater the power that can be produced by straightening it; furthermore, the greater the distance covered by the pushing blade and the shorter the time in which it is covered, the greater the power produced (assuming that the amount of the skater's weight going into the push is constant). These facts have definite implications for skaters interested in developing more stroking power.

First of all it is absolutely necessary to develop a really deep skating knee bend, which means that the legs must be strengthened so that the body weight can be supported on a deeply bent knee. Second, a really rapid straightening action of the pushing leg must be developed.

Leg Lifts

One leg

An excellent method for strengthening the legs is to practice the leg lifts as follows—skate forward a few strokes to get some speed, then glide on two feet in a straight line, extend arms out in front, bend knees deeply and go down in a squat position and sit on heels, (hint—thinking of placing chest on knees as you go down helps keep weight over center of blades). Next, slide one foot out in front of you. After you have glided in this position, return the front foot to its original place beside the other foot and come back up on two feet to a standing position. Repeat with other foot in front. When you can accomplish

Touch ice doing
alternate sculling
or scooters.

this with ease, on either foot, it's time to start doing the whole exercise on one foot. Start with a one foot glide on right foot, bring left foot forward and go down on the right leg as far as you can, glide a short distance and come back up to standing position still on the right foot. Keep practicing until you can go all the way down and come up again on one leg. You may find at first you will have to put the other foot down in the process of going up or down, but if you practice this every time you skate you will be surprised at how soon you will be able to do it on either foot, without help. You can then proceed to do as part of your warm-up every time you skate a set of 3 to 5 leg lifts on each foot. Instead of going down and up once, go down-up—down-up three or four or more times on the same foot for each exercise This is guaranteed to strengthen your legs for stroking, jumping, and all skating.

For increasing the speed of the pushing thrust, some of the two-footed exercises explained in chapter IV can be used to your advantage. For instance, the scooter drills where the pushing is done only with one foot while the other foot stays on the flat of the blade (skater travels straight path) or on an edge (skater travels circular path) are very effective. Try the straight scooter first. Keep left foot on flat of blade and push with right foot only. At start of push bend both knees deeply, straighten right leg as rapidly as possible when thrusting with the inside edge of blade. Lift right foot at end of thrust and repeat. Be sure to maintain or increase the knee bend of the left leg during the push otherwise the distance covered by the push will be cut short. A good way to work on increasing the speed of the push is to start with a count of four for the push, then reduce the count to three, then two, then one, while keeping the distance covered by the push the same. Repeat using left foot as pushing foot. Try also on curve—put nonpushing foot on an outside edge. Keeping the inside hand touching the ice will force you to bend the inside knee to its maximum.

Alternate sculling (stroking—with both feet remaining on the ice) is an excellent exercise for increasing stroking power. Since both feet stay on the ice it is feasible to increase the knee bend of the support leg to the maximum while thrusting with the pushing leg. Many advanced skaters use this as a warmup when they first go on the ice.

Crossover Strokes

Everything that has been mentioned on power stroking for open strokes applies as well to crossover strokes. In addition there are a few special points that relate only to crossover strokes. The first of these has to do with getting a power push from the outside edge of the blade; and the second has to do with keeping the strokes even.

Crossed pumping is an excellent drill for developing a power thrust from the outer edge on the forward crossover (fig. 22). In this drill the feet remain crossed all the time and all of the pushing is done by the back foot as it moves out and forward pressing with the outside edge of the blade against the ice. To do this drill, begin with a few strokes (scooter if you like) on a circle to get moving. Then allow outside foot to go forward in front of other foot and move so you are in the crossover position. Use the outside edge of the back foot to push against the ice. At the end of the push keep back foot on the ice, but skate it forward and in towards the other foot so that it is close to the other foot, but still crossed behind it and outside of it. Push with the back foot toward the outside of the curve by aiming the toe outward, using the outside edge. Allow other knee to bend deeply in this pushing or pumping movement so back foot can stay in contact with ice.

At end of push, aim toe of back foot in again, rise up on other knee as back foot is brought close to (but still outside of and crossed behind) front foot. Continue with this in-and-out pumping motion of the back foot until you can accelerate easily. Many skaters have trouble getting started on this drill, because they try to push the back foot backward instead of out and forward in the pumping action. This drill can be used for backward crossovers also, but of course the direction of the pumping action would be out and backward instead of forward.

81

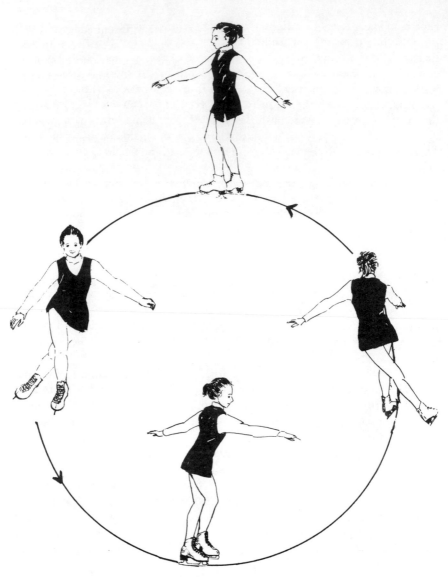

Figure 22. Crossed pumping. Both feet stay on the ice and crossed throughout the exercise. All pushing is done by the back foot using the outside edge. Forward leg must bend to allow back leg to extend outside the curve during the push.

Because skating on a curve or circle involves two different edges and two different strokes (i.e., —open and crossed), one frequently sees a very uneven type of movement, which causes one to wonder if the skater has one leg shorter than the other. As mentioned frequently before, the power for any stroke comes from the straightening of the pushing leg. If a skater, when skating on a curve, bends the knee more on the open stroke than on the crossover stroke the corresponding pushes will be uneven and likewise the resulting power. For maximum efficiency and smooth appearance the knees must bend deeply on both strokes and the thrust must be made with the same speed from the outside and inside edges. When this occurs the skater appears to move around the circle or over the end of the ice with great speed and a smoothness almost approaching a floating appearance in the upper body.

Open push   Crossover push

Two footed crossover—forward: touch ice with inside hand on every push.

A good drill for equalization of knee bend and thrust is to skate around a circle doing an open stroke then a crossover stroke, but keeping both feet on the ice at all times and really accentuating the knee bend on each stroke so that you can touch the ice with your inside hand at the end of each thrust.

Finally to develop more stroking power you must practice, practice and practice your stroking, concentrating on a quick and complete straightening of the pushing leg on every stroke (open or crossed) accompanied by a deep bend in the support leg to allow for a maximum thrust. Fifteen minutes a day of continuous stroking alternately fast and slow should produce obvious improvement in stroking powers within a short time.

CONDITIONING

Skating like jogging or swimming can be used as the medium for a fitness and conditioning program. Such a program can be set up in a variety of ways from a standardized format geared to a group of skaters to a very exact and specific interval training program designed for a particular individual. The information and suggested program presented in this chapter will enable you to establish for yourself a generalized skating-conditioning program with a means of measuring its effectiveness. If you wish to obtain a more individualized and exact program you are referred to "Interval Training" by Fox and Mathews.

Of course it is necessary for you to have already acquired the basic stroking skills before you attempt to use them in a conditioning program. If you are still having problems with balance in stroking, you are not yet ready for such a program.

Recent evidence indicates that interval training methods which incorporate alternate work and relief periods are more efficient in conditioning than continuous work periods. The reasons for this are as follows: during the relief periods the muscular energy systems are partially or wholly restored and ready for reuse thus preventing the accumulation of fatigue products and making possible a higher work intensity during the work periods. In addition, the heart muscle itself does its maximum work during the recovery period rather than during the work period, so increasing the number of recovery periods actually gives the heart more "practice" in contracting to a maximum. Over a period of time this results in more powerful individual contractions of the heart muscle resulting in a larger volume of blood being pumped through the heart with a resulting increase in efficiency.

Setting Up Your Own Fitness Program

The suggested conditioning program presented in this chapter uses the principles of interval training. The work periods are those of fast skating followed by relief intervals of slow skating. It is essential that the participant go "all out" during the fast periods pushing himself or herself to maximum speed and effort every time. Keeping records of the distance skated and time in which it is skated can be helpful in motivating a maximum effort each time by trying to lengthen the distance and reduce the time in succeeding repetitions. In the slow periods skaters can reduce the speed of the strokes but continuous stroking must be maintained . . . there should be no gliding on two feet which allows complete rest. The program starts slowly and builds gradually. Because individuals vary greatly in their general state of fitness it may move too slowly for some and too rapidly for others. It is therefore necessary to have some means of measuring the effectiveness of a conditioning program. The crucial factor is the work intensity, and a very good index of that is the heart rate. It is a relatively simple matter to count the heart rate immediately after a work interval and by comparing the results with those in table 5 to determine if a sufficient work intensity is being achieved. If your heart rate is not up to the value given in the chart for your age group you have several options. You can go ahead in the program to the second or third week and try that pattern of practice, or you can stay with the pattern of the first week but increase your speed so that you have more repetitions during the practice periods. Either option should result in increasing the work intensity to a sufficient level.

Table 1

Target Heart Rates During ITP Work Intervals
(men and women)

Age, Years	Heart Rate Beats Per Minute
Under 20	190
20–29	180
30–39	170
40–49	160
50–59	150
60–69	140

From INTERVAL TRAINING by Fox and Mathews, copyright 1974 by W. B. Saunders Company, Philadelphia, Pa.

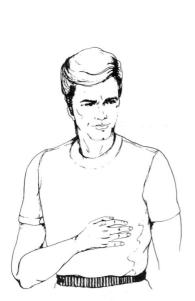
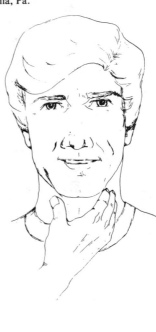

Figure 23. Pulse counts may be taken at the carotid artery (in the neck) or by holding the hand over the left breast.

Generalized Skate Conditioning Program

Daily skating is recommended. If this is not possible, then at least four times weekly should be the goal. If possible use opposite directions for first and second periods of practice.

First Week—Continuous stroking practice—3 minutes at the beginning and end of your skating session.

Pattern—One lap fast (all out) stroking followed by three laps slow . . . repeated as many times as possible in the 3 minute period.

Second Week—Continuous stroking—4 minutes at the beginning and end of your skating session.

Pattern—Same as first week . . . try to make the fast lap faster each time.

Third Week—Continuous stroking—4 minutes at the beginning and end of your skating session.

Pattern—Start with 1 lap fast and 3 laps slow, repeat once then go to one lap fast and 2 laps slow, repeat as many times as possible in the 4 minute period.

Fourth Week—Continuous stroking—5 minutes at the beginning and end of your skating session.

Pattern—Start with 1 lap fast and 3 laps slow, then 1 lap fast and 2 laps slow for the remainder of the 5 minute period.

Fifth Week—Continuous stroking—6 minutes at the beginning and end of your skating session.

Pattern—Begin 1 lap fast 3 laps slow then 1 lap fast and 2 laps slow, repeat once, then 1 lap fast and 1 lap slow for the remainder of the 6 minute period.

Sixth Week—Continuous stroking—7 minutes at the beginning and end of your skating session.

Pattern—Same as for fifth week.

Seventh Week—Continuous stroking—8 minutes at the beginning and end of your skating session.

Pattern—Begin 2 laps fast, 4 laps slow—repeat twice then 1 lap fast 1 lap slow for the rest of the time.

Eighth Week—Continuous stroking—9 minutes at the beginning and end of your skating session.

Pattern—Begin with 2 laps fast and 6 laps slow (once), then 2 laps fast and 4 laps slow (twice), then 2 laps fast 2 laps slow for the remainder of the time.

Ninth Week—Continuous stroking—10 minutes at the beginning and end of your skating session.

    Pattern—Begin 2 laps fast 1 lap slow (twice), then 2 laps fast 2 laps slow, (twice), then 2 laps fast and 3 laps slow the remainder of the time.

Tenth Week—Continuous stroking—10 minutes at the beginning and end of your skating session.

    Pattern—Same as for ninth week.

In order to carry out this conditioning program it is necessary to be consistent in performing the practices, daily if possible. After the first week you should check to see if you are obtaining a sufficient work intensity. This can be done by checking your pulse rate immediately following a work period. Pulse rates are most easily taken at the carotid artery in the neck or by holding the hand over the left breast. Use a stop watch and count for a 30 second interval then multiply by two and compare the result with the rates listed in table 5 for your age group. If you are more than a few beats below the rate listed in the table you will need to push yourself to a more intensive effort. Have someone time your fast laps for you and then set out to improve your times. From week to week you should be able to discern a progressive drop in your best time for a single lap and for double laps. Faithful practice during the conditioning program will result in an increased cardiovascular efficiency and significant improvement in leg strength and endurance.

Supplemental Readings

Fox, Edward L. and Mathews, Donald K.—1974—"Interval Training," The W. B. Saunders Company, West Washington Square, Philadelphia, Pennsylvania 19105.

Melograno, Vincent J. and Klinzing, James E.—1974—"An Orientation to Total Fitness," Kendall/Hunt Publishers, Dubuque, Iowa.

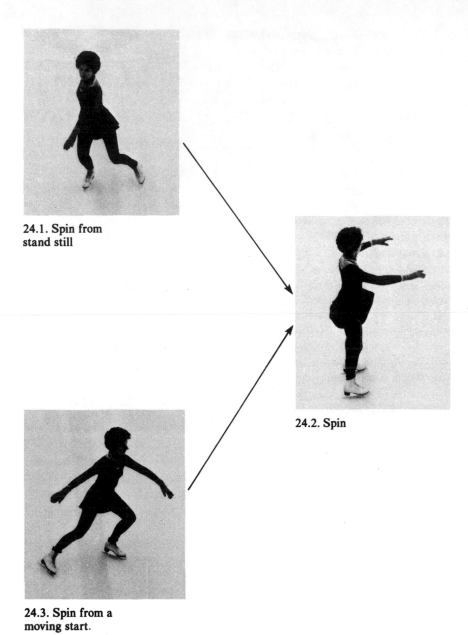

24.1. Spin from
stand still

24.2. Spin

24.3. Spin from a
moving start.

Figure 24. Two foot spin.

Chapter VIII

Some Elementary Figure Skating Skills

SPINNING

Most people are fascinated by the spinning skater on the ice. With a little patience and instruction almost anyone can learn to do it. Even if you get dizzy at first, your body will gradually learn to tolerate the motion if you persevere. Keep dizziness to a minimum by holding the head straight, eyes looking out rather than down. Do not try to focus on anything in particular. Keep eyes open but do not try to 'spot' as in dance.

Steps to Spinning*

1. Determine if you have a natural direction of rotation by turning yourself easily with your feet, first to the right then to the left. If one direction definitely feels better, then that is the way you should spin. If it doesn't seem to matter, then spin to the left as that is the more common direction. Your jumps should be matched to your spin direction. If you spin to the left then you will jump from left to right.

2. Learn to spin on two feet first, because you will have a broad base of balance and can learn to feel the balance points on the blades as well as the direction of movement of the edges on a small centering circle.

3. Start the spin from a standstill, arms extended to sides, hands in front of line of shoulders. For a spin to the left, (reverse directions if you spin to the right) turn shoulders a quarter of a turn to the right and bend knees deeply (Fig. 24.1). You can anchor left toe pick in ice to keep hips from turning. To start the turning-rise up by straightening knees as you turn shoulders back to original 'square' or neutral position and bring right hand toward left, release left toe pick and let momentum of upper body, arms and shoulders be carried through to skates. Turn toes in slightly with feet on inside edges, one moving forward one moving backward on your centering circle (Fig. 24.2). At first leave arms extended so you turn slowly and stay in one spot. After you can stay centered begin bringing arms in (elbows 1st, then forearms crossed) *slowly* to keep spin going. Don't

---

* (Description is given for spins to the left (rotation is counterclockwise). Reverse all left and right terms in the description for spins to the right (clockwise).

bring arms in too quickly at first as it will cause you to spin too fast, lose control and get dizzy. The object when you are first learning is not to spin *fast*, but rather to turn slowly on one spot and feel balanced. Once you have your balance and can center the spin you can start bringing the arms in faster. The faster you pull them in the faster you will spin.

After you can do 3 turns from standstill without travelling you should try to spin from a moving start.

4. Spin from a moving start

Glide on two feet on a small curve to your left with arms extended. Left foot must be on good outside edge. Push to the side with a sculling motion of the right foot. Simultaneously bend the left knee deeply as you center your weight over it and increase the edge and curve. Now bring the right foot forward on the ice in a wide arc around the left foot as it turns from forward to backward and rise up into the spin by straightening the left leg. This start will give you more momentum going into the spin. The important thing still is to "center" the spin and get the feeling of your feet moving on inside edges on the centering circle. Your right foot will be moving forward and your left will be moving backward. Eventually you will spin on one foot, the left one, and you will be spinning on the inside back edge.

5. Transition to a one foot toe scratch spin.

As your two foot spin develops you can gradually start putting more weight on the left foot and let the weight shift a little more toward the front of that blade, so that you find the balance point where both the blade and the 1st tooth of the toepick are contacting the ice. When you find this balance point, you will be able to find a double track on the ice and to hear the sound of the scratch of the toe. Be sure to stay on the blade as well as the pick. (The most common problem is to lift too high on the pick and then you cannot stay balanced.) Gradually transfer all of your weight to the left foot and lift right foot completely off the ice.

6. One foot spin—from a T position

Once you can shift your weight entirely to your left foot in the two foot spin and find the correct balance point, you are ready to begin work on a one foot spin. Start in a T-position left foot in front with arms extended to either side and hips and shoulders square (at right angle to the front foot). Take a good left outside forward edge on a well bent skating (left) knee with the free leg held well back. Hold the edge around past 180° and increase the degree of curve,

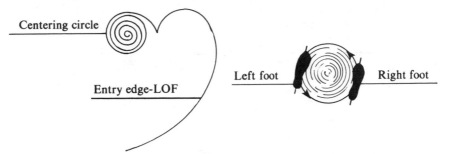

Centering circle

Entry edge-LOF

Left foot

Right foot

B.1. One foot spin on the left foot. Entry edge if LOF. Spin is done on the centering circle of LIB. Circles get smaller as spin goes faster.

B.2. Two foot spin to the left-centering circle. Right foot moves on IF left foot moves on IB on the circle. Feet come closest as spin winds up—circles get smaller.

Skater spinning on centering circle.

so that you are pressing around in an ever tightening curve (i.e., a spiral) (Dgrm. B). Next bring the right leg and foot forward as you rise to the front of the blade to the balance point involving pick and edge and begin to spin on the inside back edge and first tooth of the pick. Keep hips level when bringing free leg forward.

Beginners may find it easier to bend the knee of the free leg and bring the free foot beside the skating knee at first, then down beside the skating foot as the spin progresses. Later when balance is better it can be fully extended in front. Use arms as in the two foot spin.

7. One foot spin—from back crossover

Move backward slowly in a counterclockwise direction. Cross right foot over left on deep back inside edge with upper body turned to right (Fig. 25.1) bring feet together as upper body rotates back to left. Step into center of curve on deep left outside forward edge with arms out to either side and good bend in skating knee, right leg held well back. Hold edge around past 180° then bring right leg forward as you rise up into spin.

As your spin improves you can start bringing the free foot in to the skating knee (by bending free leg at knee, do not move upper free leg) and then bringing it down on the other side of the skating leg so feet are crossed at end of spin. (Fig. 25.4).

8. Checking out of spins

Checking out of a spin is very similar to checking out of a jump, and the smart skater realizes that he can gain valuable practice for jump landings by utilizing a good position on checking out of spins.

To check out of a spin open arms out to sides (keep hands in front of line of shoulders), bring feet close together and push out with the left inside back edge to the right outside back edge with left leg moving on through to be carried in back and a little to the side (Fig. 25.6). Keep hips and shoulders level and square to skating foot.

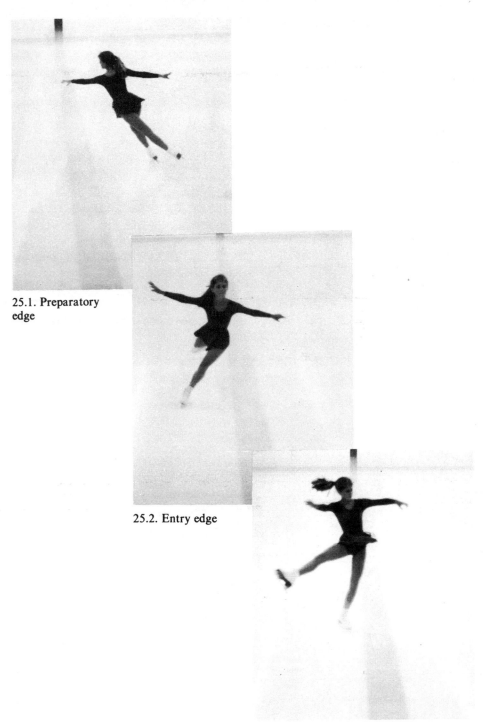

25.1. Preparatory
edge

25.2. Entry edge

Figure 25. One foot spin.

25.3. Centering

Figure 25—*Continued*

25.6. Checking out

25.5. Windup
(front view)

25.4. Windup

THE FOUR BASIC EDGES

You have already learned that every skate blade has two edges running along its length (the inside edge nearest the big toe side of the foot and outside edge nearest the little toe side of the foot). You have learned how to use these edges in stroking, stopping and turning. Now it's time to consider a different meaning for the word edge in skating. It is also used to apply to the curve that is made when you lean to one side and skate on just one edge. Since the blade has two edges and you can move either forward or backward, there are four possible edges to be skated as follows: outside forward, inside forward, outside back, inside back. When you add the factor of right and left feet the sum total of possible edges you can skate on becomes eight. i.e., right outside forward (ROF), left outside forward (LOF), right outside back (ROB) etc. . . .

A fundamental part of figure skating is learning to use and control these edges which form the basis for all figure skating. In order to do this you must be able to hold certain body positions when skating an edge. This holding of position is made difficult by the strong tendency of the body to turn into the direction of the curve when the skate is placed on the edge. This tendency is known as 'swing', and it occurs on all edges. It is therefore a central problem of control for skaters. Certain body positions can minimize or counteract 'swing', in fact, each edge has a position which gives maximum control for a particular move.

In describing these positions we shall distinguish between the skating foot (the support foot) and the free foot (the foot that is off the ice), and we shall extend these terms to the other parts of the body. Thus if you are skating a right outside forward edge your right foot is your skating foot, your right shoulder is your skating shoulder, your right hip is your skating hip, etc. The terms front and back refer to the front and back of the skater's body. When you skate any of the four edges, it is necessary to keep your skating hip pressed in tightly under you and to keep shoulders and hips level in all positions.

1. Outside Forward Edge (Fig. 26.1)
    Notice the upper body is turned outward from the curve bringing the skating shoulder and arm forward to lead. The skating arm is held in a comfortable natural curve across the front of the body. The free leg is carried behind with the free foot close to the ice and slightly inside of the curve. The whole body inclines slightly to the center of the circle. Shoulders and hips are level, but because of the body lean the free side is a fraction higher.

    A good way to begin is with a forward scooter (pumping with the outside foot around a circle—the inside foot rides on an outside edge). Reverse the usual crossover position of the arms by turning the upper body outward and taking the just described outside edge position of shoulders and arms. After you have acquired some speed and lean into the curve pick up the pushing foot and carry it in the

95

26.1. Outside forward
edge

26.2. Inside forward
edge

26.3. Outside back
edge

26.4. Inside back
edge

Figure 26. The four basic edges.

position described for the outside edge. Hold the edge and position as long as you can. You will probably find that at first the free foot and shoulder will want to 'swing' forward, but as you practice you will discover how to use the muscles of the hip and back to counteract the swing.

Practice this starting position for the forward outside edges on both the right and left foot. Later you will want to do consecutive edges and then it will be necessary to learn additional positions. The outside forward edge is very important for jump take-offs and entry into spins.

2. Inside Forward Edge (Fig. 26.2)

The upper body and hips face along the curve in a position square to the skating foot. The free arm is brought forward on a slight curve across the front of the body. The skating arm is extended out to the side with the hand forward of the shoulder. The free leg is carried slightly inside the curve in an easy position with the toe pointed down and back.

Start by gliding forward on a curve on two feet. Place arms in the forward inside edge position and lift inside foot to proper position. Hold the inside forward edge and position as long as you can. Practice on both right and left foot.

3. The Outside Back Edge (Fig. 26.3)

This is the edge on which most jumps are landed. So learn it first in jump landing position. Notice arms are extended to either side with hands held in front of the line of the shoulders. The hips and shoulders are square to the skating foot. The back is flat rather than arched with the torso inclined slightly forward from the hip joint to place head over toe of skating foot. The skating knee is well bent. The free leg is extended back and slightly to the outside of the curve. The head is erect and looking forward.

Begin with a backward scooter—arms extended as indicated above. When you have acquired some speed and lean pick up outside foot and extend it behind and slightly outside of the curve. Hold position on a well bent skating knee as long as possible.

4. Inside Back Edge (Fig. 26.4)

For a beginner the most important position for this edge is the checked position used after three turns. The upper body is turned in to the curve with the skating shoulder pressed forward; this brings the skating arm in front of the body and skating hand inside the curve. The free shoulder is pressed back taking the free arm back with the hand slightly outside curve. The free leg and hip are pressed back and free foot is outside the curve.

Begin with a backward scooter upper body in crossover position. Glide on two feet on the curve after you have gained some speed, turn the upper body a little more into the curve and lift the inside foot. Carry it outside the curve by pressing free hip back and bending the free knee. Hold in this position as long as possible. Hint: Be sure to keep skating hip tight and pressed in under you and keep skating foot fairly upright—any collapsing of the ankle on to the edge will give too much edge and will force you to fall off of it.

BEGINNING JUMPS

All jumps require a bend in the knee of the jumping leg on take off to provide lift, and a bend in the knee of the landing leg to cushion the impact of the landing. Lift in jumps comes from the thrust of the takeoff leg, the throw of the free leg, the depth of edge and the arms. It is better to work on position and control of landing at first and then later try for height on jumps. For jumps involving rotation it is necessary to learn to 'check out' of the jump in a good landing position. The descriptions are given for jumps going from left leg to right leg and where rotation is involved, for those jumps turning to the left. If you spin to the right, you will want to jump the opposite way (from right to left) so it will be necessary for you to reverse all left-right terms in the descriptions.

It is very important to have good fitting skates with strong built in support when you are jumping. If you are renting skates or have no support in your own skates just walk through the jumps or hop them. Use the correct positions for take off, flight and landing, but do not try to really jump until you have good strong skating boots.

1. Bunny Hop

   A forward leap from one skate to the toe pick of the other. Start by moving forward on the flat of the blade (left foot) with left knee well bent. Throw right leg forward as you lift the left heel and spring up from left toe pick. Land on right toe pick and push off immediately to left foot on flat of blade. Incline upper body slightly forward at take-off (Fig. 27.2) and keep hands low and forward. (This insures that the body weight is going forward off the front of the skate at take-off.) Bend left knee well on landing.

   Before doing the jump from a moving start it is a good idea to do it from a standstill to practice the landing and get the feeling of lift. Do not swing the free leg forward in this case, just bend the knee and lift the foot straight up so it's right under you for the landing. Be sure your pick comes straight down in to the ice for the landing.

27.1.

27.2.

27.3.

Figure 27. The bunny hop.

2. Toe Hop

A half turn jump with a toe pick assisted take off. Start by moving backward on the right foot, bend right knee and extend left leg backward. Place left toe pick in ice and simultaneously push up with right leg and pull with left leg in a scissors motion to lift you up over the left leg which acts like a vault. As you take off into the air turn the body a half turn and land forward on the right pick and push immediately to the left foot. This jump can be done in a straight line, but it works better on a curve.

28.1.

28.2.

28.3.

Figure 28. The toe hop.

3. Waltz Jump

A half turn leap from an outside forward edge on one foot to an outside back edge on the other. For the take-off a strong outside edge position is needed with the skating shoulder leading and the free leg, arm, and shoulder all held back. As the skating leg straightens in the thrust for take-off the free leg is thrown forward as the arms lift to aid in getting height in the take-off. The legs are straight in flight (Fig. 29.2) and the landing is made on the ball of the foot on the outside back edge with the knee bending to accept the body weight. The landing position for this jump is very important because all backward landing jumps will use this edge and position. Notice (Fig. 29.4) the arms are extended to either side, the free leg is back and slightly outside of the curve, the knee is well bent, the back is straight and the head is looking to the front. This edge and position cannot be practiced too much.

When you begin, it is good to do the jump from standstill from a T position. Push on to the front foot with the skating shoulder forward, free arm and free leg back, move the free leg and arm forward as you make a small hop to the other foot landing backwards, with the arms out to the sides and the new free foot extended behind, slightly to the side of the skating foot. In the air the arms come to a rounded position in front of you and the legs are both extended. It is helpful to walk through the three positions (Fig. 30) for the take-off, flight in air and landing without jumping. Then when you find those easy add a hop and still later a real jump. Eventually you will go into the jump from a preparatory outside back edge.

4. Toe Loop

A full revolution jump with a toe assisted take-off. The take-off is like that of a Toe Hop. Right foot on the outside back edge with the left leg extended in back in order to place the toe pick in the ice. Use a scissor motion of the legs (push up on right and pull to left) in the take off. Turn a full turn in the air and land on the ROB in the same landing position as the waltz jump.

Begin by doing the jump from standstill with a slight cheating action. Arms should be placed in an L position, left arm forward right arm to the side. Shift weight to left toe and hop over to the ROB edge.

Next—begin the preparation for the jump with a RIF 3 turn done on a very slight curve. Be sure to check after the 3 in an L position. Gradually try to eliminate any turning on pick. Use a scissor motion in the take off and turn the whole turn in the air.

29.4. Landing—extension

29.3. Landing

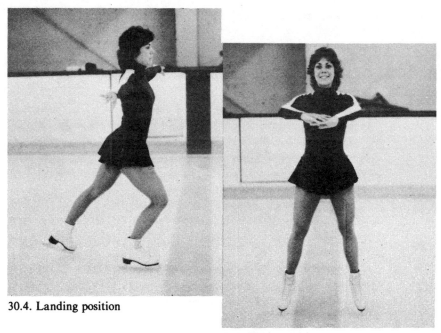

30.4. Landing position

30.3. Flight position

29.2. Flight

29.1. Take-off

Figure 29. The waltz jump.

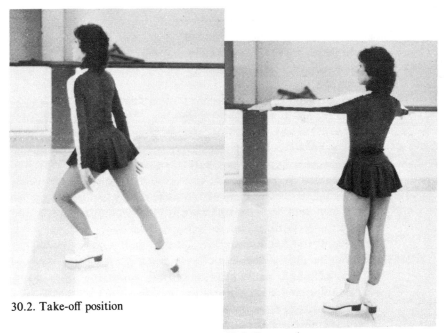

30.2. Take-off position

30.1. Preparation

Figure 30. Walking thru the waltz jump positions.

Figure 31. Spiral.

SPIRALS AND PIVOTS

1. Spirals

The natural path of the skate is a spiral one. If you hold an edge long enough it will show a spiral pattern. Hence, long edges held in definite positions are known as spirals. Most frequently one sees spirals held in an arabesque position (Fig. 32) but there are also standing spirals.

It is a good idea to do a lot of stretching before you attempt a spiral. For most people the "hamstrings" behind the knees need stretching. One way to get this stretch is by hanging forward from the waist and letting everything stretch out as you reach for the ice. Do not bounce in this position just let the weight of the body slowly cause the stretch. Hold for a count of 30–50, rest—repeat 5 times.

Next practice your spiral position holding on to barrier. Be sure to keep head up and back arched. The point of balance on the skate for a forward arabesque spiral is back quite far toward the heel. The skating leg is straight and locked and you have the feeling of riding the heel of the skate. Try to point the toe of the free foot out and back for a really nice line in your spiral. Try the spiral in a straight line first, arms out to sides. It is easier to hold this position at speed so stroke down one side and across the end of the rink then do your spiral down the other side.

Figure 32. Outside back pivot.

2. Pivots

A pivot is a skating move in which one foot is fixed and the other foot circles around it.

The inside forward pivot is the easiest one to learn. Skate forward on the inside edge on a small curve—reach wide into the circle with your free foot and place the toe pick in the ice as an anchor keeping most of your weight over the moving foot and circle around the anchored foot.

The same type of pivot can be done on the inside back edge.

The outside back pivot is more difficult and more interesting to do. You can begin at the barrier. Stand with your right hand nearest the barrier. Put your left leg back behind you and turn the ankle so that the outer edge of the blade is near the ice and anchor the outer edge side of the toe pick (Fig. 33). Turn right toe till it faces the barrier and put right blade on outside edge. Make sure shoulders and hips are level. Keeping weight mostly over right foot push away from barrier and ride the OB edge around to barrier on other side of back foot. Repeat but move a little further out from barrier and try to go around twice. To perform the pivot away from the barrier you must get on an ROB edge (from a RIF 3 or back crossover). Move the free arm forward and reach back with your free foot into the circle. Let the left toe move lightly over the ice (on the outer edge side) and gradually anchor it and pivot around it. Keep most of your weight over the moving foot and make sure the shoulders and hips stay level.

Appendix A

Definitions

Parts of the Skate

 rocker—the curvature of the bottom of the blade from front to back

 counter—the built in support in the instep of the boot

Mechanics

 center of gravity (c.g.)—the point through which the resultant force of gravity acts on a body, or the point at which the entire weight of the body may be considered to be concentrated.

 line of gravity—a line formed by dropping a vertical line downward from the center of gravity. The closer that line falls to the center of the base of support the more stable the object will be.

Edges

 edge—one of the two actual edges running along the length of the blade or the curve made by skating on one of those edges.

 outside edge—the actual edge of the blade nearest the little toe side of the foot, or the curve made by skating on the outside edge of the blade.

 inside edge—the actual edge of the blade nearest the big toe side of the foot, or the curve made by skating on the inside edge of the blade.

 flat—blade is vertical causing both edges to be in contact with the ice.

Body Positions

 square—the horizontal line of the shoulders and hips is at right angles to the line of the feet (drawn from toe to heel).

 parallel—the shoulders and/or hips are rotated toward the line of the feet.

 front and back—always refer to the anatomical front and back of the body of the skater.

 inside or outside foot—always refers to the anatomy of the skater relative to the center of the curve being skated. Thus in a crossover the outside foot is crossed in front but is still designated the outside foot.

 check—the process of stopping rotation in a turn, spin or jump by means of holding a particular body position counter to the pull of the rotation.

Descriptive Terms

free foot—applies when the skater is on one foot. The foot that is off the ice is the free foot and that side of the body is designated as the free side.

skating foot—when the skater is on one foot the support foot is known as the skating foot and that side of the body is known as the skating side.

Skater's 3-Minute Warmup

3–Minute warmup for Skaters (done off-ice before putting on skates)

60 sec.	jog in place
20 sec. A	achilles stretch (10 sec. each leg)
60 sec. B	front thigh stretch (30 sec. each leg)
20 sec. C	knee bounces* (10 sec. each leg)
20 sec. D	ankle rolls ** (5 each direction on both feet)

A

B

C

D

*Knee bounces—back leg bends and straightens in soft bouncing action—front foot acts as stabilizer—weight is centered on back leg.
**Ankle rolls—rotate foot in a circle first in an inward direction 5 times, then in an outward direction 5 times.

Appendix C

Blade Mounting

Blades should be mounted on a line which is either parallel to or coincident with the center line of the boot. The center line of the boot is one which connects the midpoint of the front of the boot with the midpoint of the back of the boot. Since boots have an irregular shape a method is needed to determine the two necessary midpoints. The following lines present one such method.

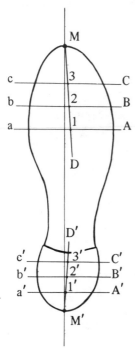

1. Draw a straight line (Aa) across the widest part of the front of the boot.
2. Draw two more straight lines (Bb, Cc) that are parallel to Aa.
3. Find the midpoint of Aa on the boot. (1)
4. Find the midpoints of Bb and Cc on the boot. (2 and 3)
5. Draw a straight line through points 1, 2, and 3 to the tip of the boot to point M which is the midpoint of the front of the boot.

Repeat exactly the same five steps on the heel of the boot to find the point M'.

6. Connect the two points M and M' with a straight line. This line MM' is the center line of the boot.

Figure i.

Figure skaters often like their blades set to the inside of the center line . . . it becomes a matter of individual preference. Hockey blades are riveted on at the factory and cannot be moved, so it is a good idea to check the blade placement before buying. Blades on speed skates are offset to the left on both skates.

Skate Sharpening

Skate blades should be kept free of nicks and burrs and edges should be maintained by adequate sharpening. Both hockey and figure blades are hollow ground which means that the surface of the blade between the two edges is concave. It is most important that this concavity is symmetrical. If it is not, one edge will be higher than the other and the skater will have all kinds of difficulty. If you have figure skates, it is important that whoever sharpens them does not change the rocker (shape of the curve on the bottom) by using uneven pressure from front to back, or grind down the first pick. Most rinks have at least one person who specializes in sharpening figure skates, and it is a good idea to inquire about this possibility. Skates that have been well sharpened hold edges beautifully but do not grab the ice with a razorlike cut. Super sharp blades are difficult to skate on and make stopping a near impossibility. If yours come back in that condition, ask the operator (or you can do it yourself) to take a piece of fine (00) emery paper and go over each edge once (one way only) to take the super sharpness off . . . then go out and enjoy skating again!

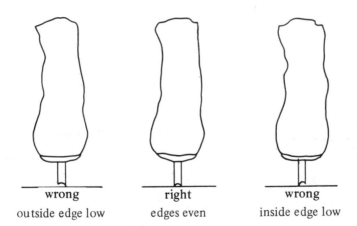

wrong	right	wrong
outside edge low	edges even	inside edge low

Figure ii. Skate sharpening.